Enlivenin
Chakra of the Heari

The Fundamental Spiritual Exercises of
Rudolf Steiner

Florin Lowndes

SOPHIA BOOKS
Rudolf Steiner Press

Translated by Matthew Barton

Sophia Books
Rudolf Steiner Press
Hillside House, The Square
Forest Row, East Sussex
RH18 5ES

First Published by Sophia Books 1998
Second edition 2000
Reprinted 2001, 2005, 2009
(Sophia Books is an imprint of Rudolf Steiner Press)

Originally published in German under the title
Die Belebung des Herzchakra, Ein Leitfaden zu den Nebenübungen Rudolf Steiners
by Verlag Freies Geistesleben, Stuttgart in 1996

A catalogue record for this book is available from
the British Library

ISBN 978 1 85584 053 9

Cover by Andrew Morgan
Typeset by DP Photosetting, Aylesbury, Bucks.
Printed and bound in Great Britain by
Cromwell Press Group, Trowbridge, Wilts

Contents

PART THREE: THE HEART EXERCISE

PART FOUR: THE NEW HEART-THINKING

Preface to the English Edition

For some time now, the nature and beneficial uses of the chakras—for instance, awakening them through meditation or utilizing them for healing—have been the subject of widespread interest outside the New Age movement. Most, if not all, of this work has revived age-old methods of practice from the eastern esoteric tradition, especially those of yoga. However, a crucial, though perhaps not immediately apparent, question regarding these practices arises: do traditional methods, even though certainly appropriate and effective in the past, really meet the actual spiritual goals and the truly modern consciousness of the present?

Today any serious spiritual seeker interested in chakra work must ask this question in spite of the widespread acceptance of these traditional methods—or rather just because of it.

As first-hand experience demonstrates, traditional yoga practices can claim certain benefits; however, experience also shows that such older forms, even when 'modernized', are not fully consistent with a truly modern consciousness and subsequently are not, so to speak, at the cutting edge of the New Age. We can find an authentic modern way of working on the chakras in the exercises created by Rudolf Steiner (1861–1925), who, on the basis of a new kind of thinking process, recast certain yoga exercises in a form consistent with the modern and even future stages of (spiritual) development. In this way, he fulfilled a small and little known branch of yoga meditative practice, the Gayatri-Sadhana, the goal of which was prophetic, for it was focused on the reversed Kundalini (awakening the energy of all seven chakras from top down instead of the usual upward method) in a way that had become possible only at this much later historical time.

This book is concerned primarily with the group of exercises Rudolf Steiner created for enlivening the *chakra of the heart*, generally known as the 'subsidiary', 'supplementary' or 'accompanying' exercises. In it appear the contents of workshops on enlivening the heart chakra that I gave in the United States and Germany. I started off in these workshops with just a couple of handouts for the participants. These handout sheets gradually became more and more detailed and their number kept increasing, until they were eventually incorporated in a slim handout volume on the method I had developed for carrying out these exercises. Then I was encouraged by my publisher, well aware that a systematic approach to these was not available, to prepare an edition suitable for general publication. So, to the best of my ability, I refashioned and expanded the material from the living oral form it took in my workshops into its present written form. But this is not easily done, since any method of practice, being intended for individual practitioners, must invariably take on the very specific character best suited to the individual who applies it. Yet any method, when it is put into written form for a wide readership, inevitably assumes a more general and theoretical character and consequently may be perceived as a composition of rigid and dogmatic directives.

I always tried in my workshops to open myself to the questions and specific needs of individual participants, and thus to allow the workshop to emerge accordingly.

Therefore, I ask my readers to view these descriptions mainly as suggestions and stimuli, and to relate them to their own particular circumstances and actual capacities. The method described here will be of no use if it is applied in an abstract, lifeless, or dogmatic way. I conceived the present volume as a 'do it yourself' kind of book for those who actually will do the exercises, rather than for those merely interested in piling up knowledge about them—for, as the saying goes, 'if you don't do what you know, you don't know it.' Nothing would bring me greater satisfaction than if this book would help its readers to develop their own individual techniques.

What I have been able to share in the seminars is the result of decades of involvement both with the exercises themselves and with the spiritual principles underlying them, as well as with the laws at work in the way they are carried out. From the beginning of my work, I have been fortunate to have followed the clear and decisive direction pointed out to me by George O'Neil (1906–88). In following this path, I have recognized that these exercises had been created by means of a *new kind of thinking*, one which ultimately offers us the only means of enlivening the heart chakra in a way thoroughly consistent with its essential function for our times. Rudolf Steiner designed these exercises for the enlivening of the heart chakra in such a way that, in doing them accordingly, we will gain access to the creative power of a truly modern thinking process, namely, 'thinking with the heart' or heart-thinking. With this phrase, I do not mean the kind of feeling way of thinking that might first come to mind, but I use it rather as a technical term (hence the hyphenated spelling), the meaning of which will be explained and justified in the last part of this book. Suffice it to say, this is the kind of thinking that we desperately need to develop today, and by enlivening the heart chakra we will actually develop its proper physical organ. For the true organ for heart-thinking is indeed the heart (not the heart muscle *per se* but the rhythmical flow of blood regulated by it), just as its supersensible organ is the heart chakra.

This book was originally intended as the second of two about heart-thinking, the first of which was to describe its nature and outline and appropriate methodology. However, this book, the second of the series, now appears before the first, which will be published in Germany this year (1998). And yet this sequence, as it turns out, is appropriate: since these exercises are better known to many readers than the kind of thinking which underlies them, this book can serve as good preparation for the more 'basic' one. It has been an important concern of mine to place the exercises described here into the context of today's widespread interest in the chakras, and thereby to show that Rudolf Steiner's approach is truly modern and it can speak to a broad range of people. I hope, therefore, that this book can be of real value to those who are currently pursuing such meditative exercises from all sorts of different traditions, especially because it seeks to reveal the fundamentally new kind of thinking on which all truly modern spiritual work must be based today in order to become truly fruitful.

PART ONE:
THE CHAKRAS

1

The Method

I would like to begin by describing a few aspects of what underlies and constitutes this path for developing the heart chakra. Any reader who is interested only in carrying out the exercises themselves can skip to the second part of the book without more ado; whoever would prefer to understand their organic, living complexity, and their effects, should read these introductory chapters. Let me also suggest here that putting aside any preconceived notions about the whole subject under discussion will make it easier to grasp properly some of the perhaps unusual or unfamiliar aspects involved.

Wherever feasible I have given my observations in a schematic or tabular form, rather than as description, for it seems to me that this would leave the reader freer to expand it into a form suited to his or her own inclinations and experience.

Viewpoints

The exercises will be examined according to the following viewpoints:

1. as exercises for enlivening the heart chakra (chakra exercises);
2. as a renewal, for our times, of an esoteric path of self-development;

3. as a field of activity of soul-forces and adversarial forces;
4. as self-sufficient, dynamic meditation (the complete exercise);
5. as expression of the organic-living thinking developed by Rudolf Steiner;
6. as examples of the lack of clear definition in spiritual experience.

1. The chakras are organs of the invisible, spiritual bodies, or energy-bodies, of the human being. They developed throughout human evolution, firstly by *natural* means, secondly through conscious, focused esoteric training. Such training can speed up the development of these organs, so that they forge a path upon which natural evolution can follow. Rudolf Steiner mentions an esoteric training for developing the chakras in some of his early writings and lectures; in his book *How to Know Higher Worlds*, and at other places, he speaks about the special evolution of the heart chakra, which he regards as being the chakra of greatest significance for our time.

2. In our present times we can, if we look to their original sources, find two esoteric paths of development: one has emerged from the traditional, ancient, though *renewed* path; the other is a truly new path. The first began with the Kali Yuga epoch (its first phase was yoga) and is nowadays in decline; for thousands of years this schooling took place in secret, select esoteric circles, but now its traditions have crumbled away and dispersed into common knowledge so that it has become more and more exoteric. The second path, began at the end of Kali Yuga, is by nature not a secret, occult path, but only remains hidden—that is, esoteric—because most people seeking a modern path of self-development have not yet found it (see the sketch). This path of training is really an 'open secret' in Goethe's sense, a secret revelation. It is simultaneously *eso-*and *exo-*teric, and accords with the Age of Light, the Satya Yuga.

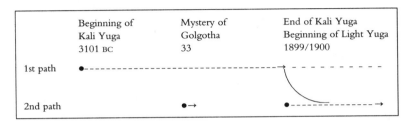

The so-called 'esoteric path' of Rudolf Steiner—first described in *How to Know Higher Worlds*—has, since the new possibilities for self-development have arisen, become a round-about route which no longer leads directly to the goal. The second path is the direct one for our times, but therefore also a steep and arduous one. The exercises described in this book really belong to the renewed first path. But as a consequence of his experiences with the new path, Rudolf Steiner formed the exercises in such a way that they create a bridge which can lead us over from the renewed to the really new path. In the chapter 'Rudolf Steiner's Two Paths of Esotericism', I will attempt to substantiate this point of view.

3. The exercises in this book relate to the human soul-forces as they are viewed in Rudolf Steiner's anthroposophy: thinking, feeling and will. They relate also to the sevenfold nature[1] of the human being, and to the effect of the trinity of adversarial forces—Lucifer, Ahriman and the Asuras.

4. In their relationship to one another and in the context of the interconnections described here, the exercises are seen firstly as six separate exercises, then as a complete exercise-organism. This organism is seen as a *single* self-contained exercise, as a *dynamic* meditation for enlivening the heart chakra—not, in other words, as a 'subsidiary' exercise.

5. The organism of six exercises is developed on the underlying foundation of organic-living thinking, heart-thinking—the thinking carried out with the heart chakra. This kind of thinking, which goes beyond the scope of normal, logical thinking, was first developed consciously by Rudolf Steiner and first introduced to the world in his *Die Philosophie der Freiheit*[2] published in English under the following titles: *The Philosophy of Freedom; The Philosophy of Spiritual Activity;* and *Intuitive Thinking as a Spiritual Path—A Philosophy of Freedom*. The exercises have therefore been developed through the application of such thinking, but they are at the same time a means for developing it in oneself.

6. In the course of the book there may be much that strikes the reader as uncertain or unclear, especially where the effects of certain spiritual beings are described. But we must remember that the exercises, when properly carried out, bring us either consciously or unconsciously to the threshold of the supersensible, and even beyond it into the world of spirit. Experiences which we have within the familiar world of the senses can rightly be assessed by means of the concepts and principles of normal, logical thinking—this is the realm in which we can have absolute certainty in exploring suppositions and actual effects. But such thinking and its attendant methods cannot be applied to the experiences which we have at or beyond the threshold of the world of spirit, in the supersensible realm. The processes and elements of this world—to which the chakras and their activity belong—cannot be determined or measured with such precision, cannot be grasped and described with such exactness. The phenomena Rudolf Steiner described in his scientific research of the supersensible world should also be viewed according to the 'uncertainty principle' formulated by Werner Heisenberg in 1927. For in observing the realm of the chakras, we find a similarity to the realm of particle physics to which this principle applies. In fact the two realms only differ from each other by a slight degree of the finer materiality still pertaining to those realms. The 'uncertainty principle' states that both the location and the energy of a particle cannot be determined within accurate limits at the same time. Rudolf Steiner was also concerned with the limits of exactitude in observing phenomena in the supersensible world, when he spoke of the impossibility of observing and thus determining precise boundaries of those phenomena.[3] This important proviso, intrinsic to the method of Steiner's science of the spirit, was mentioned by him in a lecture about human life-stages, in connection with the seven-year phases—a realm, in other words, in which the supersensible manifests within the sense world without, however, revealing its essential nature.

★

The method used here has its foundation in Rudolf Steiner's organic-living thinking. Inasmuch as this kind of thinking is based not on the brain and the nervous system but on the physiology of the heart/lung system, it is a *heart-thinking*. Rudolf Steiner spoke of the laws of such thinking only rarely and in an oblique way; they were then thoroughly explored by George O'Neil, and put together in a detailed and systematic way by myself.

Organic-living thinking is connected with the inner

constitution of the human being, as described in *Theosophy* (in the chapter titled 'The Being of Man'). For this book, only the sevenfold structure of the sheaths of the human being will be referred to, consisting of: physical body, etheric body, astral body, and ego-organization or 'I'[4] as core of the soul, spirit-self, life-spirit and spirit-man.

'I'-level	*'I'-organization*	
Astral level	astral body	spirit-self
Etheric level	etheric body	life-spirit
Physical level	physical body	spirit-man

This structure manifests a regular, symmetric and rhythmic form on four levels: physical, etheric, astral and spiritual or ego-level. The organism of the six exercises is built up on this basis, in harmony with the basic laws of living organisms—rhythm, polarity, intensification and inversion (turning inside-out).

The elements on the right-hand side arise through the ego-organization transforming those on the left. On the three lower levels there are always two aspects in a polarity to each other, and simultaneously in a relationship to one another of inner/outer or outer/inner:

outer/inner—the three bodily sheaths as expression of the inner spirit sheaths;
inner/outer—the three bodily sheaths as inwardly concentrated core (personality), and the three spirit sheaths as outer cosmic beings (individuality, entelechy).

The three soul-forces of the ego-organization—thinking, will and feeling—show their effects on the three levels in the following way: thinking in the physical body, feeling in the astral body, and will in the etheric body. Of the three adversarial forces, Lucifer works at the astral level, Ahriman at the etheric and the Asuras at the physical level. (These interconnections will become clearer in the course of the book, especially in the chapter 'Structure' and in Part Four.)

'I'-level		
Astral level	feeling	Lucifer
Etheric level	will	Ahriman
Physical level	thinking	Asuras

From a methodological point of view, the question about a teacher appears to be important, especially when one considers the warnings which Rudolf Steiner gives in *How to Know Higher Worlds* (in the chapter on the effects of initiation, and in the Postscript). Should people who are working at developing the chakras, and who do not as yet have any faculties of higher perception, entrust themselves to a teacher who has these capacities? Such a question will rightly occur to the readers of this book, but I would like to underline the fact that I do not see myself in any such role—I am simply speaking of my own experience. In the final chapter, though, I will try to answer this legitimate question and justify the method I describe.

The bodies of the human being—two approaches

Of the above-mentioned sheaths constituting the human being, only the *physical body* can be perceived by our normal sense organs; it is therefore seen as belonging to the sense world, while the other sheaths, perceptible only to higher, supersensible organs, belong to the supersensible or spiritual world. These supersensible sheaths can therefore only be seen by a clairvoyant, someone who possesses such organs of perception. As well as the physical body, anthroposophy also calls the two next sheaths 'bodies'—*etheric body* and *astral body*—for they have a direct influence on the physical body's organs and functions. As such, they operate within the realms of space and time and partake of materiality, even though in a highly rarefied form, rather like a high potency in homoeopathy. One can also speak of an *ego body*, or *'I'-body*, which is likewise formed within spatial conditions, but in this case can be experienced as negative space, as vacuum devoid of matter. The sheaths above these are of purely supersensible or spiritual nature; they can no longer be thought of as bodies but as soul or pure spirit sheaths.

The three spiritual bodies appear to clairvoyant vision as increasingly spreading out beyond the physical body. (The following is only a brief summary, sufficient for the purposes of this book. For a more thorough and detailed description, see *Theosophy* and *How to Know Higher Worlds*.) The etheric body is perceived as a light-form, composed of continually vibrating, oscillating, interpenetrating streams of energy. It is similar to the form of the physical body, but somewhat larger, spreading a few centimetres (about one inch) beyond the surface of the skin. The astral body appears to the clairvoyant as a cloudlike form of light and colour, roughly in the shape of an egg, about twice as high and broad as the physical body which is at its centre. The ego body does not occupy a particular form as such, but manifests as negative space, vacuum, a hole, rather like a 'sun-space' as Rudolf Steiner terms it, or also as a glittering, shining, constantly self-recreating, pure light that radiates out beyond the astral body (see Fig. 1).

Although only a clairvoyant can perceive these super-sensible bodies, everyone can on occasion have some experience of them. This can happen in extreme situations, in which our life-forces or emotions or sense of self are threatened (at times of severe illness, for example, or in states of emotional or existential crisis). It is a common experience during illness that our life-forces are not suffi-cient to 'fill' the whole body, and at such times we can feel ourselves smaller—the physical body seems to shrink. The opposite happens when we feel good—after a particularly refreshing holiday perhaps, or after invigorating physical exercise when we can feel 'bursting' with energy, even to the extent of sensing this energy as a real tingling spreading out from us through our skin. At times of sorrow or soul-pain many people can sense their astral body as a dark, thick cloud, usually in the upper part of the body, in the chest and head regions. When, in contrast, we are full of joy, we can experience a bright, radiant kind of feeling, as though the upper part of our body is permeated by beautiful colours and light.

In a similar way we can have a sense or inkling of our own ego body—for example when we wish to express our conviction about something, or want to say sorry, and accompany our words by touching or tapping a particular point of the body. Then we can sense the centre of our own being as a particular point deep inside us in the heart region (see Fig. 2).

Perceiving the supersensible bodies can therefore happen in either one of two directions: from within outward or from outside in. In the first case we begin from the physical body, from its centre as though from a point, and perceive

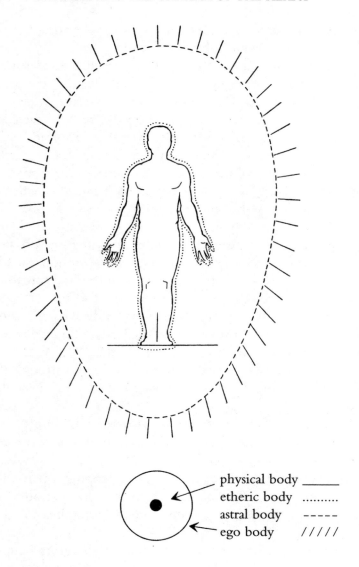

physical body _____
etheric body ....
astral body -----
ego body /////

Fig. 1: Aura of the three bodies

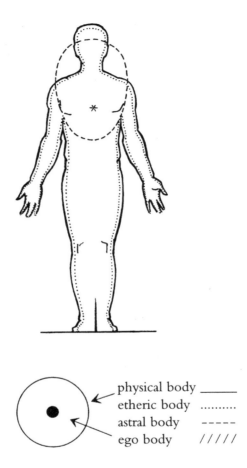

physical body _____
etheric body ....
astral body - - - - -
ego body / / / / /

Fig. 2: The three bodies within

the other bodies encircling and enveloping this point. In the second case we sense the supersensible bodies as increasingly diminishing, until we arrive at the central point, the ego body. These two directions of perception, in line with the 'uncertainty principle', correspond with the reality of these bodies, for they can simultaneously be found both within and outside of the physical body. The totality of the supersensible bodies is known as the 'aura', which takes account of the clairvoyant's point of view, point → periphery, whereas an ordinary person's experience of differing degrees of well-being are expressed in the direction of periphery → point. The exercises described in this book can only properly be grasped when we understand the nature of this polarity between inner/outer and point/periphery.

★   ★   ★

2

The Traditional Chakra Teaching

This chapter aims to give a brief but, for the purposes of this book, sufficient overview of the chakras, in order to place what I have to say into a broader context. Throughout I will use the term 'chakra', except in quotes from other sources which use different expressions.

There is now a wealth of literature available on the chakras, which has arisen through the searching of ever greater numbers of people for supersensible experience. This literature originates almost exclusively from the chakra teaching of oriental tradition. The work I wish to describe, though, points in a different direction.

Rudolf Steiner's science of the spirit, or anthroposophy, points us towards the future, yet he nevertheless makes some mention of this traditional chakra teaching. He referred to it at the beginning of the twentieth century, above all in the context of his spiritual-scientific activity within the German section, which he founded, of the Theosophical Society. In 1904/5, in his periodical *Luzifer-Gnosis*, he published a series of essays, subsequently collected together in book form (1909) as *How to Know Higher Worlds*. The main thrust of this book is concerned with certain exercises for developing the chakras, so as to gain knowledge of higher worlds in a way suited to our present stage of human evolution.

Rudolf Steiner's chakra teaching differs considerably in this respect from other approaches current nowadays. These actually only lead back to a recapitulation of ancient knowledge and have only limited value—relevant especially to the area of spiritual healing. Rudolf Steiner based his chakra teaching on the foundations of his previously developed *new thinking*, while the eastern traditions perpetuated in the West are rooted in the habitual forms of thinking. (This theme will be dealt with at more length in Part Four of this book, 'The New Heart-Thinking'.)This is the significant difference. Rudolf Steiner only related the outer form of his chakra teaching to tradition, while actually basing it on quite new foundations dictated by the needs of the future. If we know how to recognize this difference, then a chakra teaching is also indispensable for anthroposophy—but it must be one that is grasped in a quite different way from ancient tradition. (The reason, perhaps, that most people who become involved in Rudolf Steiner's anthroposophy show no interest in the chakras is that the subject has not yet been properly explored.)

In the decades since *How to Know Higher Worlds* was published (the last edition overseen by Steiner himself appeared in 1922), real progress has been made in investigating the chakras and their role. This is due to the fact that many people in the West explored the subject—either through their own direct experience or, in small numbers, by applying modern principles of science to this area of supersensible experience. In particular, the work of Valerie Hunt, an American, should be mentioned. In the 1970s and 1980s she carried out research at the University of California, and was the first to use exact scientific measurements to prove the physical and energy effects of purely spiritual processes to be identical with the chakra-perceptions of clairvoyants.[1]

In this section I have taken account of various works in

this field—especially *Hands of Light* by Barbara Ann Brennan[2]—because they seemed to me to demonstrate a balanced approach underpinned by scientific method. I have also referred to *The Chakras* by Charles Leadbeater, because it was influential at the time *How to Know Higher Worlds* appeared, and because Rudolf Steiner himself made reference to Leadbeater's clairvoyant drawings.

What are the chakras?

The chakras are organs common to the supersensible bodies; they interfuse these bodies and have a particular task in each of them. They arise wherever certain streams of energy consistently intersect one another. Within a body, or a level, of the aura they manifest as force centres that provide the energy necessary for it, and regulate its functions.

In the etheric body the chakras support the life-force and the energy necessary for maintaining the functioning and health of the physical body. Each chakra provides a supply of energy for a particular part of the body and its organs, including the endocrine glands, the nerve ganglia, etc. At this level the chakras regulate the life processes—they are the spiritual organs of life, or *life-organs*.

In the astral body the chakras support the development of the various aspects of consciousness—not only self-awareness but also higher, supersensible consciousness. The development of the chakras creates the basis for gaining knowledge of the higher, supersensible world and its beings. At this level the chakras are *spiritual organs of spiritual perception*.

At the level of the ego-body, they unite in the rays that create the vibrational structure for expressing the spiritual individuality.

'Chakra', which in Sanskrit means 'wheel', is today the most common term used in specialist and popular literature for denoting these organs. (In Indian esoteric tradition the chakras were often represented symbolically as lotus blossoms, and also given this name. In the American traditions of the Incas and Aztecs, they were called 'flowers'. Rudolf Steiner usually used the term 'lotus flowers' rather than 'chakras'.) In the literature on the subject, three kinds of chakras are distinguished: 7 main chakras, 21 secondary chakras, and a great number of little chakras (up to 88,000)[3] which give rise to the well-known acupuncture meridians. In the present context only the main chakras will be considered.

The chakras appear to clairvoyant perception as concentration or interference points in the energy streams, in a form similar to a funnel or a flower calyx, and always with a particular number of continually vibrating 'petals' of a particular 'colour'. These formations are joined through a lengthening of their tip to the main energy stream from which all the chakras arise, and at their other end they open at the surface of the etheric body or in the various layers of the astral body (see Fig. 3). These openings are described by most clairvoyants as appearing at particular points on the surface of the etheric body, about one inch (2.5 cm) above the surface of the skin and have a diameter of about six inches (15 cm). They have a flower or wheel form, and are subdivided into several 'petals' or 'spokes'. Barbara Brennan says of these petals (or 'vibrating fields' as Leadbeater calls them): '. . . These petals appear to be small vortices rotating at very high rates. Each vortex metabolizes an energy vibration that resonates at its particular spin frequency.'[4] The chakras can best be classified by the number of these petals.

Chakra in the
adult

Chakra in the
child

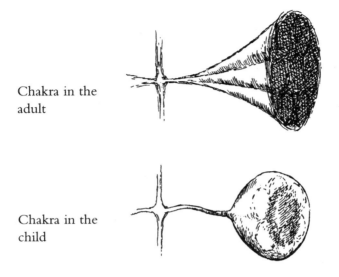

Fig. 3: Chakras in the adult and in the child (after Brennan)

The seven chakras are distributed over the etheric body as follows:

1. The *four-petalled chakra* (root chakra) lies at the base of the coccyx and opens downwards towards the earth's centre of gravity.

2. The *six-petalled chakra* (sacral or sex chakra) lies in the region of the lower abdomen and reproductive organs and opens horizontally at the front and back of the body (this is also true of the 3rd, 4th, 5th and 6th chakras).

3. The *ten-petalled chakra* (solar plexus chakra) lies in the region of the navel and the solar plexus.

4. The *twelve-petalled chakra* (heart chakra) lies in the heart region.

5. The *sixteen-petalled chakra* (throat chakra) lies in the throat and neck region.

6. The *two-petalled chakra* (forehead chakra)—which is

actually composed of two groups of finer petals consisting of 48 petals each (96 altogether)—lies in the middle of the forehead between the eyebrows.

7. The *thousand-petalled chakra* (crown, or top-of-the-head chakra)—which is actually composed of two groups of petals, a larger consisting of 960 and a smaller of twelve-petals (972 in total)—is situated above the apex of the head, and opens towards the heights of the cosmos.

In Figs 4 and 5 the chakras are depicted according to Barbara Brennan's latest description and Charles Leadbeater's portrayal from the beginning of the twentieth century. The following observations relate especially to these illustrations.

Different clairvoyants inevitably perceive different aspects, according to their particular capacities for super-sensible perception. As is apparent from these sketches, the descriptions are different and often contradictory. We are therefore not seeking a single, generally valid, 'objective' depiction of the chakras, for the 'uncertainty principle' is at work here. Nevertheless, the different descriptions do come fairly close to reality.

Leadbeater's sketch, one can see, is rather less precise than Brennan's. This may lead us to conclude that after nearly a century research has become more exact, systematic and scientific.

Although Rudolf Steiner did not give any pictorial representations of the chakras in *How to Know Higher Worlds*, he pointed out that Leadbeater's illustrations could well be used to augment his own descriptions.

The form of the chakra organism illustrated here has been adopted more or less by everyone studying the chakras, and simply transposed in the same form upon the astral body level. But this organism has another, additional

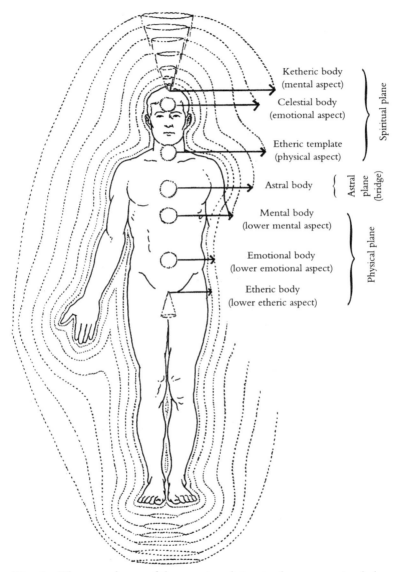

Fig. 4a: The seven layers of the aura in relation to the seven main chakras (after Brennan)

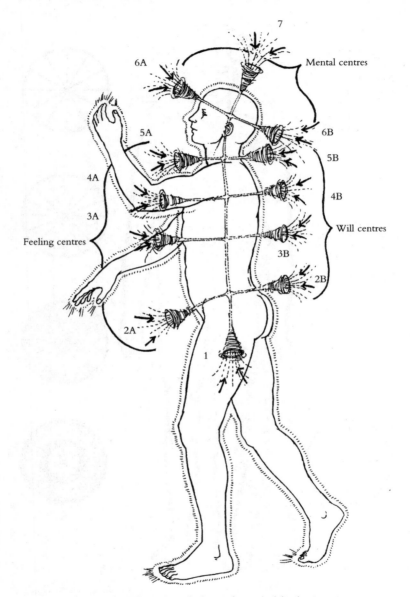

Fig. 4b: The seven chakras, front and back view

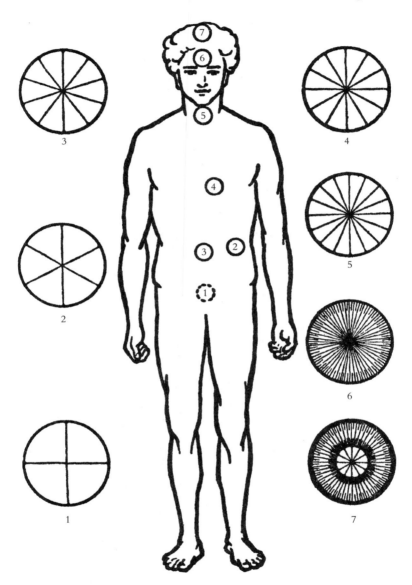

Fig. 5a: The seven chakras according to Leadbeater

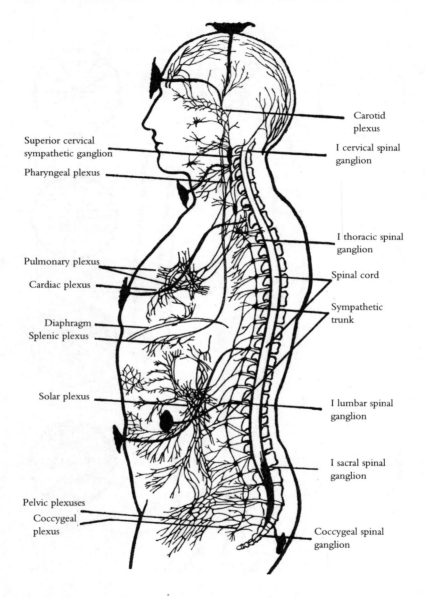

Fig. 5b: The chakras and the nervous system according to Leadbeater

structure, which is of decisive significance for the evolution of the chakras at the astral level—for spiritual life as such—both now and in the future. This structure is mentioned to my knowledge only by Rudolf Steiner and will be examined in the context of the next chapter.

The kundalini

The chakras are united by streams of energy, called 'Nadis' in Sanskrit. Some ancient Indian and Tibetan texts speak of 72,000 Nadis, while others say there are 350,000.[5] All these streams are joined together in a central, unifying form; two streams flow in opposite directions towards one another in a serpent-like meander, the whole maintaining its direct connection with the field of universal energy by means of a central, upright stream. When the energy field of the chakras culminates through the two 'snakes' at the highest point, and the central stream *flows up forcefully from below*, in other words, passes from the centre of gravity through the root chakra up to the crown chakra at the top of the head, and then on and beyond it, we speak of the awakening of the *kundalini*. In Sanskrit this term means roughly 'coiled or rolled up like a snake'. Once awoken, this snake ('snake-fire' in Leadbeater, 'kundalini-fire' in Steiner) becomes upright and active. Figure 6 can give us an idea of this, and shows us at the same time the origin of the well-known image of the Mercury staff. The wings of the Mercury staff point to the elevation of normal consciousness to higher, spiritual vision, which also shows us the deeper meaning of medicine—real healing only comes about when earthly consciousness becomes spiritualized.

This activation of the kundalini can occur gradually or very suddenly, and brings about a spiritual awakening, a

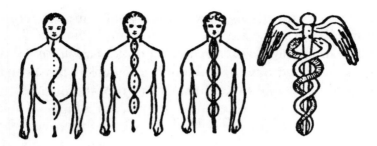

Fig. 6: The three main streams of the chakras, and the Mercury staff

conscious entry into supersensible realms. This awakening leads on the one hand to an ecstatic experience of the supersensible world (clairvoyance), and on the other to the development of the physiological basis for modern consciousness. This comes about through the opening or activation of the crown chakra, which previously enabled the brain to evolve to its present form. (Pursuing this theme in greater depth would go beyond the scope of this book. In passing I can only mention that we are concerned here with the 'holographic' structure of the universe, and with the brain as a mirror of the universe—a concept that has been developed by various scientists working in different though connected fields, such as Bohm, Pribam and Gabor. Through research such as theirs ever more scientists are coming closer to grasping in their own terms the realities described by Rudolf Steiner.) The crown chakra was therefore seen as the most important one, and simultaneously as the centre of the whole chakra organism, for it forms and directs the brain and the head, our central organ as thinking earthly beings.

The difficulty for advanced esotericists of today is to translate what they perceive through an expanded consciousness into the normal thinking of ordinary consciousness.

The first half of chakra evolution took place at the level of the etheric body, and is now complete. The second phase of this evolution began at the turn of the nineteenth to the twentieth century, and takes place at a higher level. But describing it in the right way, once it has been perceived, requires the right concepts, and these can only be formed through a new kind of thinking.

The further evolution of the chakras will take place at the astral level, and in the reverse direction—*from above downwards*. One can therefore speak of the *reversed kundalini*. (The awakening of the kundalini from below upwards takes place largely in the etheric body, and therefore leads to an ecstatic kind of experience rather than to clear, thinking consciousness and knowledge.) This reversal will give rise to a new human physiology and consciousness. This means that the 'universal life-energy field' will spread down from above—in other words, from the world of spirit through the crown chakra firstly, and then on through the whole body as spiritual-astral stream, as conscious activity of the astral body. So when the spiritual fire-force enters us through the top of the head, no longer through the coccyx and the sexual organs, then the creative, procreative energy which now underlies earthly life will be replaced by the higher energy. Then the image of Whitsun will become reality: the spirit flaming above the head of every single individual human being. The further evolution of the chakras is directly related to the impulse instigated by the Whitsun event; its time has now come. Rudolf Steiner's chakra teaching should also be seen in this light.[6]

★   ★   ★

3

Rudolf Steiner's Chakra Teaching

There are three chief aspects which distinguish Rudolf Steiner's chakra teaching from other, traditional chakra teachings. In the following two chapters I will clarify and elaborate these three aspects, drawing particular attention to the special role of the heart chakra and to why enlivening it is of such importance for our times. The heart chakra will therefore occupy the central place in these discussions; the other chakras will be dealt with only in connection with the heart chakra and the exercises that belong to it.

In *How to Know Higher Worlds*, Steiner describes a path of schooling and self-development for our time. This path aims to form and structure the chakras as higher, supersensible organs of perception, as sensing organs of the soul, of the astral body. 'Until we have developed the astral senses in this way, we cannot see anything supersensible.'[1] This path begins with the higher chakras, in contrast to the traditional path leading from the lower to the higher ones. The first decisive difference, therefore, is that in *How to Know Higher Worlds* Steiner describes the 'Christos path' and does not simply go back to the ancient, traditional path.

In the relevant chapter, 'Some Effects of Initiation', Steiner twice mentions the sequence of the chakras: he first describes their position in relation to the parts of the physical body, and he then describes a new 'focal point' of the etheric body in the region of the physical heart as follows:

These organs—which we shall now consider—may be seen spiritually in the following areas of the physical body: the first, between the eyes; the second, near the larynx; the third, in the region of the heart; the fourth, in the neighbourhood of the pit of the stomach or solar plexus; and the fifth and the sixth, in the lower abdomen or reproductive region.[2]

The twelve-petalled lotus flower is closely related to the central point described above. All the currents flow directly into and through this 'point'. Thence, on the one side, some currents continue up to the sixteen- and the two-petalled lotus flowers, while on the other, lower side, they flow down to the eight-, six- and four-petalled flowers.[3]

Both times, as we can see, *six* chakras are mentioned, though not exactly the same ones in each case. Neither passage refers to either the thousand-petalled or the ten-petalled chakra of the traditional chakra sequence. Instead a different chakra is mentioned: the *eight-petalled*. An eight-petalled chakra is known of in writings on the subject, but it is a 'secondary chakra' (Leadbeater) rather than a main one. Steiner therefore also describes a sequence of seven chakras in total: the two-petalled, the sixteen-petalled, the twelve-petalled, the ten-petalled, the eight-petalled, the six-petalled and the four-petalled. Thus his sequence, or chakra-organism, is a *different one*. That is the second difference.

The third aspect is connected with the 'focal point' mentioned above. This will develop in the future once a group of new etheric organs have formed in the etheric body, for:

Further esoteric development, therefore, consists precisely in adding to those movements of the ether body, which are independent of our consciousness, currents and movements that we ourselves have consciously produced.[4]

These currents and movements belong to the new chakras in the etheric body and the vibrations caused by them, which correspond to the new chakras developed in the astral body.

By the time esoteric training has reached the stage when the lotus flowers begin to rotate (or move), we have already done much of the preparatory work needed to produce certain specific currents and movements in the ether body. The goal of our development is now to form a kind of *central point* near the physical heart from which currents and movements spread in manifold spiritual colours and shapes. In reality, of course, this centre is not really a 'point', but rather a quite complex organ ... the more developed a person is, the greater the circumference formed by these spreading currents.[5]

That is the organ that will in future unfold and form the new centre of the whole human organism, assuming the central task which the brain still fulfils nowadays. The connection of all the chakras to this focal point will not directly emanate from each individual chakra, but will *take place through the heart chakra:*

This arrangement accounts for the fact that, in esoteric training, especially careful attention is paid to the development of the twelve-petalled lotus flower. If any mistake is made here, the development of the whole system is thrown into disorder.[6]

We can now see why the heart chakra has such a central place among the other chakras, and therefore why the exercises for developing it are of such importance. Carrying out these exercises will systematically help the etheric streams unite with the newly forming centre, for this is already present in us in embryonic form. We will look at this in more detail in the next chapter, and also at the importance of these three aspects or differences for the enlivening of the heart chakra.

Firstly, though, I will give a broad overview of the exercises for activating the chakras as they are described in *How to Know Higher Worlds*.

*

With the new organism of seven chakras, Rudolf Steiner set the parameters and aims for the modern and also future path of chakra development, at the same time giving the exercises corresponding to it. These will now be briefly described:

The two-petalled chakra

A direct exercise is neither described nor hinted at. But the whole book, as well as the relevant chapter, underlines the importance of clear thinking. I will give just one example:

> Certain forms of clairvoyant seeing appear as the result of distortions in the development of the lotus flower. In this case, the seeing is marked not only by illusions and fantastic ideas but also by deviance and instability in daily life ... This happens particularly when not enough attention is paid to logical, level-headed thinking in the training. Of prime importance is that the student of esotericism be a sensible person, devoted to clear

thinking. Equally important is to strive for the greatest clarity in speech.[7]

The practice of such thinking therefore underpins all the other exercises. It is the inviolable precondition for the whole path.

The sixteen-petalled chakra

For this, *eight* exercises are described in a clear and systematic manner; they have a certain similarity to the traditional Buddhist teaching of the eightfold path.

> However, the point here is not to teach Buddhism but to describe conditions for development that grow out of spiritual science itself. That they agree with certain teachings of Buddhism does not make them any less true in themselves.[8]

The twelve-petalled chakra

In just as clear and systematic a way as for the previous chakra, *six* exercises are given here. Each one is also connected with a particular concept, such as 'Control of thoughts' or 'Tolerance', and the totality of the six exercises is described as the 'so-called *six attributes*'. A peculiarity of these exercises is that they are described twice: the first time as exercises for the heart chakra (the six attributes); and the second time as the *third* of the 'four attributes' formed by the eight-petalled chakra, where they are termed the 'third capacity' and listed, but not thoroughly described as they were the first time (see below). (The second part of this book deals with these exercises separately.)

The ten-petalled chakra

For this, no further exercises appear to be given. Instead, *five* specific conditions or directions are clearly but not systematically referred to. It is no longer as obvious as it was up to this point whether there are a specific number of exercises.

The six-petalled chakra
Here it is even harder to be sure whether any exercises are being referred to, because all that is mentioned are *three* fairly general principles as requirements or directions for the life of soul, body and spirit.

The *exercises* mentioned up until now are described as ones for forming the 'sense organs of the soul' or the 'lotus flowers'. For the following two chakras, the eight-petalled and the four-petalled, no exercises are either given or referred to, and no mention of these chakras is made—at least it seems so at first glance. In fact, certain exercise possibilities *are* pointed to, but these references are not to be found in the part of the chapter dealing with the development of the chakras. They are, instead, referred to in a veiled way in the section of the chapter dealing not with the astral chakras but with the higher organs in the etheric body, and in particular the central organ at its focal point. This is formulated in the following way:

> Still, something more than this assurance is needed when, having developed the six-petalled lotus flower, we begin to perceive living and autonomous beings that belong to a world very different from the world of the physical senses. The development of the lotus flowers is not enough to give us confidence and certainty in these worlds. We have to have still higher organs at our disposal.
>
> We shall now discuss the development of these higher organs before continuing the discussion of the other lotus flowers and the further organization of the 'soul body'.[9]

The enlivening of these last two chakras therefore takes place at a higher stage of spiritual schooling, and the references to it are given for advanced pupils, although they also provide beginners with a certain idea of chakra development.

The eight–petalled chakra

This chakra itself is mentioned only once, and nothing further is said about it. It seems initially as though Steiner fails to give any corresponding exercises. Yet in fact he gives *four* exercises—although they are not described as such, but as the 'four attributes that we must attain on the so-called trial path, in order to ascend to higher knowledge', and which at the same time must be 'incorporated into the soul so that they become the foundation for inner habits'. The third quality is, as suggested above, actually the exercise for the heart chakra.

The four–petalled chakra

Similarly, there is nothing in the whole chapter which relates directly to the four-petalled chakra; it is named and nothing more. Yet towards the end of this long chapter, dealing with the deeply rooted illusions or reflections in us of outer and inner reality—the earthly and spirit worlds— the *two* exercises appear. These illusions, which arise through the limitations of the human personality, must be overcome—and that is what the exercise consists of.

★

We can see from all this that in the chapter 'Some Effects of Initiation' in *How to Know Higher Worlds* suggestions are given for helping to activate the ten-petalled and the six-petalled chakras, and clear, systematic exercises are described for the sixteen– and the twelve-petalled chakras. In the books that followed immediately after this, *The Stages of Higher Knowledge* and *Occult Science*, as well as in many lectures, Steiner described *only* the *six exercises for the heart chakra*, and from continually new and different points of view. In other words, Steiner himself focused on these exercises for the heart chakra above all others. This clear emphasis, as well as the wealth of references and suggestions, shows us their importance as the exercises which we nowadays most urgently need to practise.

Finally, an overview of the different kinds of references to the chakra exercises in *How to Know Higher Worlds:*

two-petalled chakra: veiled references
sixteen-petalled chakra: clear exercises, given once
twelve-petalled chakra: clear exercises, repeated
ten-petalled chakra: indications
eight-petalled chakra: veiled references
six-petalled chakra: references
four-petalled chakra: veiled references

★   ★   ★

4

The Heart Chakra

In the last chapter we looked at the three characteristics distinguishing the esoteric path of chakra development described by Rudolf Steiner: the reversal of the sequence of activation, the new structure of the chakra organism, and the new central organ in the etheric body. Now I would like to examine these characteristics from another angle.

I

The activating or enlivening of each chakra is a process that naturally requires a good deal of time for its completion, usually more than one lifetime. The enlivening of all the chakras is therefore, in fact, a historical process stretching over several lives. For our present stage of evolution, the right path of spiritual schooling—one which aims to enliven the heart chakra in particular—should be based upon the already opened, two-petalled forehead chakra and the sixteen-petalled throat chakra. The enlivening of these chakras began in ancient times already, however they have not yet reached the same level of maturity in all people (the perfecting of all the separate chakras, as of the whole organism, still lies in the far-distant future), and therefore when one enters on a modern path of self-development one should first activate these two chakras in full consciousness.

The **forehead or third-eye chakra** was woken in the

classical Greek period. It was by this means that Aristotle was able to bring forth pure, conscious thinking and anchor it as logic in thinking and grammar in language. It is this which gave rise to our modern capacity, which we take as a matter of course, for perceiving as abstract thoughts in our soul certain spirit beings, or rather thought beings—for 'having thoughts' in other words. All modern people nowadays have this capacity for logical thinking, upon which modern society is founded, and without which it could not exist.

This seems to be the reason why Rudolf Steiner did not give any specific exercises for the two-petalled chakra, but only pointed out that clear, logical, reasoned thinking and the 'greatest clarity in speaking' was an absolute prerequisite for embarking on the path of self-development. Throughout *How to Know Higher Worlds* he emphasizes the need for applying *this* kind of thinking so that the other chakras can successfully be activated. In *Theosophy*, which immediately preceded *How to Know Higher Worlds* and serves as its introduction and basis, he showed how the *first* step on the path of knowledge must consist of mastering this kind of thinking. In the chapter 'Reincarnation and Karma', he made use solely of this normal, 'reasoned' thinking, rather than of his supersensible perceptions, to prove the reality of reincarnation and therefore of the worlds of spirit. Only after this ground had been laid could he start, in the next chapter entitled 'The Three Worlds', to describe the purely supersensible 'soul-world' and the 'spirit land'.

The **larynx or throat chakra** was awakened globally during the Christian period, particularly during the Middle Ages and the early Renaissance. From a certain point of view one can see that it was really during this time that

Buddha's teaching of compassion was adopted by a deepening Christianity, above all through the impulse of Francis
of Assisi. This does not mean, though, that Christianity
became Buddhism. In this connection one can recall
Rudolf Steiner's observations, cited in the last chapter,
about the exercises for the sixteen-petalled chakra. The
force of Christianity still really underlies modern society,
even if only in theory rather than practice, as an unnoticed
consequence of the effect produced by the sixteen-petalled
chakra. We should remember that the exercises given for
this chakra are similar to the Buddha path without being a
mere repetition of it. Rudolf Steiner intended them as a
resuscitation of past work upon this chakra, even if there are
possibly many people in whom the first level of this chakra
has not yet been activated.

The enlivening of the **heart chakra** is a task of our
present time and the near future, and represents the new
stage in a modern path of self-development. The awakening and enlivening of this chakra only became possible
towards the end of the nineteenth century, at the beginning
of the Michaelic age—to be precise in November 1879.
The enlivening or also, firstly, the awakening of the twelve-
petalled chakra is the central task of our time and the focus
of all efforts made on the esoteric path of schooling. It is
particularly at this level of chakra evolution that significant
changes in the structure of the chakra organism, and
therefore also in the physiology of the physical body, can be
expected. (I do not wish to differentiate here between
esoteric and natural evolution, for the progress achieved
through conscious, intended schooling will prepare the way
for the developments which arise in a natural way.) The
central focus of these changes is the transformation of
purely logical thinking into a wholly new kind of thinking,

characterized by Steiner in various different ways as: organic-living thinking; thinking which goes 'beyond logic'; 'thinking with the heart' or 'heart thinking', etc. The difference between the hierarchic sequence of the chakras on the truly new evolutionary path and that of the traditional path can perhaps best be shown by comparing the clairvoyant perceptions of Rudolf Steiner and Charles Leadbeater. (Both these men belonged to the leadership of the Theosophical Society at the beginning of the twentieth century, and both possessed faculties of supersensible perception.) But from their descriptions of the forms of perception that can be attained through the activation of the sixteen-, twelve- and ten-petalled chakras, it becomes clear that they are speaking of two different directions: Leadbeater of the ten-twelve-sixteen sequence, and Steiner of the reverse sequence of sixteen-twelve-ten. First, Steiner:

> The spiritual sense organ which is situated near the larynx, enables us to see clairvoyantly into the way of thinking of other soul beings. It also allows us a deeper insight into the true laws of natural phenomena, while the organ located in the region of the heart opens clairvoyant cognition to the mentality and character of other souls. Whoever has developed this organ is also able to recognize certain deeper forces in plants and animals. With the sense organ situated near the solar plexus, we gain insight into the abilities and talents of other souls.[1]

And Leadbeater:

> Then it moved on to the third [centre], that corresponding to the navel, and vivified it, thereby awakening in the astral body the power of feeling—a sensitiveness to

all sorts of influences, though without as yet anything like the definite comprehension that comes from seeing or hearing.

The fourth centre, when awakened, endowed man with the power to comprehend and sympathize with the vibrations of other astral entities, so that he could instinctively understand something of their feelings.

The awakening of the fifth, that corresponding to the throat, gave him the power of hearing on the astral plane, that is to say, it caused the development of that sense which in the astral world produces on our consciousness the effect which on the physical plane we call hearing.[2]

These two passages can easily be compared, in spite of the different viewpoints. A more detailed description of the sixteen- and twelve-petalled chakras makes the reversal of the traditional sequence even clearer:

The twelve-petalled lotus flower conveys a different perception from the sixteen-petalled one. The sixteen-petalled flower perceives forms. That is, it perceives as a form both another soul's way of thinking and the laws according to which a natural phenomenon unfolds. Such forms are not rigid and unmoving, but mobile and filled with life ... Quite different perceptions come to light through the twelve-petalled lotus flower. These may be roughly characterized in terms of warmth and coldness of soul. Seers, endowed with this sense organ, feel soul warmth or coldness streaming from the figures perceived by the sixteen-petalled lotus flower. This means that a seer who has developed the sixteen-petalled lotus flower but not the twelve-petalled one clairvoyantly perceives a kind thought only in terms of its forms described above. If, on the other hand, both organs are developed, then the seer also perceives something, which can be described only as soul warmth, streaming from the thought.[3]

II

On the oriental yoga path, the chakras are awoken and enlivened from below upwards. When the last in this sequence, the thousand-petalled chakra, opens, the kundalini also uncoils and thereby allows clairvoyant perception of the supersensible world. This process led, after lengthy esoteric schooling, to higher faculties of perception on the one hand; on the other, it resulted in the formation of the physical organ of consciousness, the brain—for the crown chakra rules the brain and its higher function, supporting the processes of thinking. The forces that brought about this thinking faculty were led upwards from below through the four-petalled root chakra to the other chakras, and therefore the organ of thinking arose upon the foundation of earth forces. As such, therefore, the brain is dependent upon the earthly realm. We can see this from the fact that normal, logical thinking deals only in concepts and ideas derived from sense perceptions. *All* abstract concepts, spiritual, moral, ideal, etc., are in fact only abstracted from sense-concepts. They originate in sense-perceptions of the natural world, to which we human beings belong. This shows us why the classical yoga lotus position requires the esoteric pupil to sit upon the ground—his root chakra must connect with the earth in order to allow the earth energy to stream into him through this chakra (see Fig. 7).

The path we need to follow today, if we are to pursue an esoteric schooling that is right for our time, is one that is no longer dependent in the same way upon sense-perceptions and the concepts arising from them. Our starting-point on

Fig. 7a: The lotus posture in yoga. Side view (after Sharamon and Baginski)

this path is really to be found where the ancient path reached its culmination—in the opening of the higher spiritual organs, right up to the thousand-petalled crown chakra. This brought about a liberation from dependency on the outer senses. The opening of the crown chakra resulted in the human brain developing the capacity, in all people, to think only in pure concepts rather than in pictures and images—the capacity for abstract thought in other

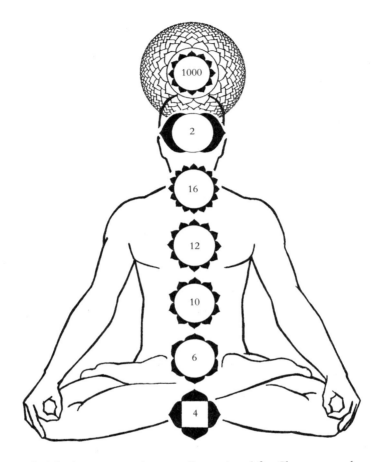

Fig. 7b: The lotus posture in yoga. Front view (after Sharamon and Baginski)

words. Once thinking in pure forms without sense-based content becomes possible, as in mathematics, we can speak of a 'pure thinking'. The world of spirit is a world of pure forms or ideas in the Platonic sense (the word 'idea' derives from the ancient Greek *eidos*, meaning form). Those who succeeded in waking the kundalini perceived this world of pure forms through their higher sense-organs, through the crown chakra, while those who cannot perceive this world yet are able to think it through the unconscious activity of the crown chakra. The crown chakra as it were replaced the earth, the ground. And the first stage on this path is the two-petalled forehead chakra as opposed to the four-petalled chakra on the traditional path. The Whitsun tongues of flame appear above our heads.

★

The vibrating energy-vortices of the thousand-petalled chakra appear to clairvoyant perception in the form of a core or kernel surrounded by 960 vortices, rather like a stigma at the centre of petals. This core was reproduced by Leadbeater in his book on the chakras, in the same shape and colour as the heart chakra (see Fig. 8 and page 200). This can lead us to recognize something which many people today have an intuitive feeling for: that the crown chakra contains a kind of duplicate of the heart chakra, a second heart chakra; that the heart chakra is concealed

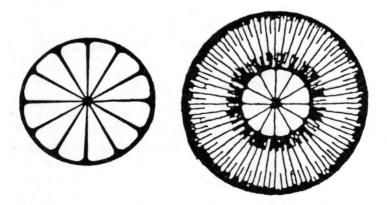

Fig. 8: Heart and crown chakra (after Leadbeater)

within the crown chakra as an *organ of thinking*. Because the direction of chakra activation is reversed, the structure of the chakra organism will also be transformed, and the heart chakra will become the conscious organ of the new kind of thinking. The reversed kundalini path, or the Whitsun path, causes the thinking heart chakra concealed within the crown chakra to situate itself first in the forehead chakra, and from there to pass through the throat chakra into the chest region where it will reintegrate in the actual heart chakra. The heart chakra will then be recognizable as a metamorphosed or inverted crown chakra.

In connection with the first steps in initiation, Rudolf Steiner spoke of a 'kind of etheric heart' that develops above the top of the head, where it can be perceived clairvoyantly (see Fig. 9). It is a kind of organ of thinking, which enables us to 'imbue with heart what we recognize through the science of the spirit'.[4]

★

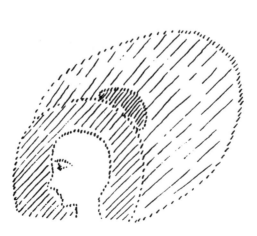

Fig. 9: Position of an etheric heart (after Rudolf Steiner)

Rudolf Steiner often drew attention to this thinking organ in the breast, sometimes in veiled references, sometimes in fairly clear and direct form. His listeners at the time—perhaps because these things were new to them—showed little understanding for the fact that Steiner saw the supersensible chakras as concrete realities. They seemed to grasp them more in a poetic or sentimental sense, and therefore as merely abstract. By now, though, we should be able to recognize that these descriptions were meant in a quite concrete way. The chakras should be understood in terms of a spiritual physiology—and also as a scientific physiology, for the physical heart will transform itself as a result of becoming an organ of thinking.

The following excerpts are just a few of the numerous references in Steiner's work to the heart as an organ of thinking. They stretch from the time of publication of *How to Know Higher Worlds* (which appeared as separate essays in 1904/5, and in book form in 1909) to the last article he wrote in 1924. Even when Steiner was speaking of things far removed from the chakras, and almost diametrically opposed to them, such as epistemological questions, his descriptions and ideas were always underpinned by supersensible processes in the inner constitution of the human being. These passages are of course lifted out of their context, but this does not alter their general validity.

We touch here on a deep mystery: the law of metamorphosis of the organs. The whole of human evolution passes through a transformation of human organs ... the heart will become the brain of the breast, will become an organ of consciousness.[5]

The head with the brain is only a transitional organ of perception and knowledge. The organ which will furnish us with really deep and at the same time powerful insights into the world has its potential seat in our present heart. Please note, though, that I say *potential*. In order to become an organ of perception and knowledge, the heart will need to be transformed in a radical way. But this heart is the source and fount of future human evolution. When the heart becomes such an organ, perception and knowledge will be warm and inward, as only love and sympathy are nowadays.[6]

True human love is rooted in the spirit ... Wherever such love is truly avowed and truly received, impulses will invariably be present which prepare the way for a real logic of the heart. The logic of thinking can lead to the greatest egotism. The logic of the heart is capable of gradually overcoming egotism and making all people part of an all-encompassing human community.[7]

Just assume you could think in a pure flow of thought. Then there will come a moment for you when you have developed your thinking to a point at which it no longer needs to be called thinking at all. In the twinkling of an eye—or let us say in the twinkling of a thought—it has become something else. This thinking—rightly called 'pure'—has become pure will; it is will through and through. If your soul-life has advanced to the point at which you have liberated your thinking from outer perception, then it simultaneously becomes pure will. Your soul-life floats, if I may put it like this, in a pure stream of thought ... Pure thinking, and even the effort to practise it, begins to be not just a thinking exercise but an exercise of will, and one which reaches deep into the centre of yourself. For you will notice something curious: that only now can you really say that you experience *ordinary* thinking as an activity of the head . . . for previously you only knew this in an external way through physiology, anatomy, etc. But now you inwardly sense that you no longer think so 'high up', but that you have begun to think with the breast. Your thoughts truly interweave with the processes of breathing, and you thereby stimulate in yourself something which the yoga exercises strived artificially to attain.[8]

The Michael Age has begun to dawn. Human hearts begin to think.[9]

III

The new etheric organ in the heart region will evolve as a result of the enlivening of the twelve-petalled and the eight-petalled chakras in particular. The heart chakra will provide the initial impulse, which will be brought to maturity through perfecting the eight-petalled chakra. This points us to a particular connection and collaboration between these two chakras.

We have already mentioned this connection in passing. You will recall that in esoteric tradition the eight-petalled chakra assumed the position of a secondary or subsidiary chakra. But in the future, through its conscious enlivening, it will take on the role and task of a main chakra. The eight-petalled chakra therefore seems to encompass something of the true nature of the heart chakra, also when it appears as main chakra next to the heart chakra in the astral body. In addition the enlivening of this eight-petalled chakra will occur as a direct result of the heart chakra's own enlivening, for of the 'four attributes' which contribute to the enlivening of this chakra the third is actually the totality of the six exercises for activating the heart chakra. These connections endowed the whole chakra organism with a pronounced heart character and quality, which also imbues the etheric organ.

In one of his 'esoteric classes', Rudolf Steiner spoke of 'ten energy centres' in the human being. The one in the chest region concentrates within itself the energy of the general life principle, the spiritual power of life, known in esoteric tradition by the Sanskrit term *prana*. Steiner explained that 'prana corresponds to the eight-petalled lotus flower'.[10] The eight-petalled chakra will contribute this prana to the perfecting of the central etheric organ, while the heart chakra facilitates the connection between this etheric organ and the chakra organism. In this way a new centre will arise in the human being, which will overcome the dependency of thinking and consciousness on the brain and on the one-sided nature of sense-perception. In the following description, in which Steiner points to such changes, the expression 'faculty' is used for the four faculties that will enliven the eight-petalled heart chakra, and the term 'virtue' for the six exercises for enlivening the twelve-petalled chakra. (At the place where he described the six exercises, he spoke of the six 'attributes' in the soul.)

We have already discussed the six virtues (control of thoughts and actions, perseverance, patience, faith and equanimity) that combine to form the third faculty. These virtues are connected with the development of the twelve-petalled lotus near the heart. It is to this region, as we indicated above, that we must guide the ether body's current of life. The fourth faculty—that of 'desiring liberation' (love of inner freedom)—serves to bring the ether organ near the heart to maturity. Once this love of freedom has become a soul habit, we ourselves become free of all that is connected only with capacities of an individual, personal nature. We cease to look at things from our own separate, particular point of view. The boundaries set by the narrow self, which chain us to this perspective, vanish. And the mysteries of the spiritual world may enter our inner life.

This is the sought-for liberation.[11]

At this point I would like to draw attention to a particular phenomenon of our times, which seems to me to have a deeper connection with what has been said so far. An increasing number of people diagnosed as clinically dead have, after being brought back to life, reported their experiences beyond the threshold of death—so-called 'near-death' experiences. In his report on a poll in 1992, the famous opinion pollster George Gallup Jnr claimed that more than 13 million people in the US had had one or more near-death experiences. Previous scientific researches have shown that such experiences are reported all over the world, so it is safe to assume that a very large number of people have had them. The following excerpt from an interview that I myself conducted with a French woman, Yolande Eck, makes it seem very likely that the 'golden sphere' she mentions is in fact the new etheric organ. Yolande Eck perceived it after passing through an experience of the 'wheel of incarnations' and the 'alternation of life and death'—in other words, her past and future incarnations.

I climbed further down, with my back to the downward slope, and freed myself from the wheel. The wheel stayed where it was, and as I got further away from it I saw on my energy body, on my stomach, a sphere of gold. The rays from this sphere were strong and powerful; and nowadays I would call them a kind of seed energy of the human constitution, a new force as it were, a new energy centre of the human being.

Everyone has this force within them, and at that moment I thought that I could now do everything on the earth that I wished. The beings of light confirmed to me that this was so, but they also told me that it was a force with which I could do evil as well as good. I was free, they said, to do with it what I wished. At that point the golden sphere freed itself from me.[12]

In the further course of this interview, Yolande Eck told me—though this wasn't published—that Jesus Christ spoke to her in the form of a being of light. This occurred during her second near-death experience. His words, she said, had flowed or radiated out *from his heart*, like a flowing, wavelike braid or ribbon upon which she could see the words he spoke. That is real heart-speech—*Imagination* in anthroposophical terms.

★ ★ ★

5

The Exercises for the Heart Chakra: 'Subsidiary' and Basic Exercises

As we have seen, then, the heart chakra is of central importance among the other chakras: it enables us, firstly, to develop a new kind of thinking; secondly, its central function in relationship to the new, focal, etheric organ means that it has the task of forming with it the future 'centre' of the human being; thirdly, its enlivening must be the focus of an esoteric pupil's efforts and strivings if he or she wishes to follow a path that is right for our times. The exercises which Rudolf Steiner gave for the enlivening of this chakra are therefore of decisive importance for such training. And yet still today these exercises are generally regarded only as secondary ones. The reason for this seems to be that Steiner sometimes called them 'subsidiary exercises' (*Nebenübungen*) which gave rise to an interpretation that undervalued their significance. It is now of urgent importance to place these exercises at the centre of all efforts to develop higher organs of perception and knowledge. For it is highly probable that Rudolf Steiner did *not* mean these exercises to be regarded as secondary to other, 'primary' exercises or meditations. The opposite is the case, as I will show in this chapter.[1]

Of all the exercises, meditations or mantras—mantric phrases or images—given by Rudolf Steiner, these six exercises were the only ones he repeatedly described in his writings and in the lectures he gave both to the general public and to the members of the Theosophical Society, as well as within his 'Esoteric School'.[2]

He focused on them therefore above all others. In *Theosophy*, he just sketched them out briefly; in *How to Know Higher Worlds*, *The Stages of Higher Knowledge* and *Occult Science—an Outline* he described them each time from a different point of view. One particular version, intended only for circulation within the inner circle of his Esoteric School, was probably written in 1906.[3] The subtitle of this version is especially noteworthy: *General requirements for anyone who desires to undertake an occult schooling*. What does this suggest? Surely the word 'general' indicates that these exercises were absolutely necessary and basic ones providing a foundation for *all pupils* and for *all other* exercises and meditations. But it was not only in his earlier lectures that Rudolf Steiner referred to these exercises more frequently and in more detail than any others. In later lectures also there are numerous references to the nature of these exercises and the principles applied in carrying them out—given from a quite different standpoint, though, so that one does not recognize them at first glance. Everything which Steiner later spoke about in this connection is also necessarily connected with the activity of the chakras in the etheric and astral body.

The term 'subsidiary exercises' must be replaced with another term which can convey the proper sense: that whenever we practise any so-called 'primary exercise', such as meditation or mantric verses—for instance, the meditations in *Guidance in Esoteric Training*—then these 'subsidiary' exercises *must* be practised alongside. They should therefore really be regarded as essential *basic* exercises, for they are of equal importance to all other 'main' exercises.

There is another reason for carrying out these exercises *alongside* other ones. One of their effects on the pupil is to protect him or her from harmful influences that are likely to arise during meditation or mantric practices. Rudolf Steiner spoke of this, for example, as follows:

Two things must once more be emphasized: firstly, that the six exercises we have spoken of paralyse the harmful influence which other occult exercises can have, so that only the beneficial ones remain; and secondly, that these exercises alone ensure the successful outcome of meditation and concentration work. However conscientiously we fulfil the ordinary moral dictates that hold sway around us, this is not sufficient for esoteric purposes, for this kind of morality can be very egotistic, leading us to desire to be good in order that others may think us so.[4]

The instant the soul withdraws part of its activity from the body, injurious powers from the elemental kingdoms may get hold of it. Herein lies a danger of higher development. Therefore care must be taken that, as soon as the soul is withdrawn from the body, the latter is in itself accessible only to good influences from the elemental world. If this be disregarded, the ordinary man deteriorates, to a certain extent, physically and also morally, in spite of having gained access to higher worlds. While the soul dwells in the higher regions, pernicious forces insinuate themselves into the dense physical body and the etheric body. This is the reason why certain bad qualities, which before the higher development had been held in check by the regulating power of the soul, may now come to the fore for want of caution. Men formerly of good moral nature may, under such circumstances, when they enter higher worlds, reveal all kinds of low inclinations, increased selfishness, untruthfulness, vindictiveness, wrath, and so forth. No one alarmed by this fact need be deterred from rising to the higher worlds, but care must be taken to prevent the occurrence of such things. The lower nature of man must be fortified and made inaccessible to dangerous elemental influences. This can be brought about by the conscious cultivation of certain virtues. These virtues are set forth in the writings on spiritual development.[5]

Steiner next describes the 'four attributes', which, as already shown above, are intended to enliven the eight-petalled chakra. But the third attribute arises from the successful practice of the six heart chakra exercises. This means that the six exercises form a part of the development of the four attributes. The exercises for the twelve-petalled chakra, in other words, are contained within those for the eight-petalled chakra. This points to the special character of the eight-petalled chakra's development: the first attribute— 'the ability to distinguish between truth and appearance'— corresponds to the clarity of thinking by means of which the two-petalled, 'third-eye' chakra should be enlivened; the second attribute—'rightly *evaluating* what is true in contrast to non-essential appearance'—corresponds to the exercises for enlivening the sixteen-petalled throat or larynx chakra—more clearly described in the form of the eight exercises for the days of the week, the eight 'right processes';[6] the third corresponds, as I have just shown, to the exercises for enlivening the twelve-petalled chakra; and only the fourth attribute—'the inner need for liberation'— appears as the *exercise* specifically directed towards enlivening the eight-petalled chakra.

Given all this, the question may well arise: If this is so, why were these exercises—in Steiner's time, and still nowadays—regarded and practised by most pupils only as 'supplementary', 'subsidiary' exercises? In what follows I will shed some light on the background to this mystifying situation, without however drawing any final conclusions. I can only unravel the few aspects of this problem which have become apparent to me in the course of my search for truth.

First of all, one can perhaps concede quite directly and honestly that the essence and all the related purposes of *How to Know Higher Worlds* were misunderstood—just as was the case with *The Philosophy of Freedom*. (A description and possible solution of this problem will be attempted by the author in another book, to which the fourth part of this present book can serve as a kind of introduction.) Such an interpretation is fuelled by a remark made by Steiner, which was passed on by Alexander Strakosch:

This occurred in 1923, at a time when certain things going on in the Anthroposophical Society were causing him concern. He asked me: 'Do you know what the difficulties in the Society stem from?' Since, understandably, I was unable to answer, he continued, 'They are caused by the fact that not enough people have attained the levels of higher knowledge described in *How to Know Higher Worlds*. When the world of spirit gave me the task of writing this work, it expected many people to go a long way on this path. So I was required to write a second volume.' Then, after a moment of most serious, silent reflection, he went on quietly: 'What was expected did not happen. The world of spirit throws out a line from time to time. This time nothing came of it ... but since there had been talk of a further book, I had at least to publish the slim volume *Stages of Higher Knowledge*.[7]

All this may lead us to the conclusion that the six exercises for the heart chakra are neither subsidiary nor main exercises, but true meditations—and of such an unusual kind that they were not perceived as such. When carried out in a manner suited to their own true nature, they achieve the remarkable effect of anchoring the pupil so that he or she keeps both feet firmly on the ground, and at the same time gradually liberating his or her consciousness from its dependency on brain-bound thinking. The special way in which these six exercises relate to one another allows a many-levelled meditative practice to arise. This is really a *dynamic* meditation which, as will be shown in the second and third parts of this volume, takes hold of and activates all aspects and bodies of the whole human being. Understandably, though, such meditation is far more difficult to perform than the 'normal' variety.

It seems that Rudolf Steiner did not think very highly of the way in which the majority of esoteric pupils practised meditation, although he never referred to this directly but occasionally allowed a hint to surface. Once, for example, in connection with a particular meditation, he warned his listeners: '. . . but it is not enough simply to theorize into the blue, which is how most people "meditate"; for the meditations of most people are nothing more than theoretical blabbering.'[8] If one does not have much success with the simpler, 'static' meditations, it will be even harder to meditate properly in a dynamic way.

This is precisely why we should take seriously the great significance and enormous worth of these heart-chakra exercises. Practising them has an effect which leads us onwards into the far, far distant future. By doing so, we help to *develop the human form for the earth's next incarnation.* It is possible that everyone senses this in their inmost soul—

along with the fear of change, which is also active within us as hindrance. It is this fear perhaps which gives rise to an unobserved antipathy towards such exercises, reinforced by sympathy for forms of meditation that seem safe and familiar. It is possible that Rudolf Steiner was addressing these deep-seated, concealed feelings when he unfurled the following perspective before the inner vision of his listeners, in the hope that it would give them courage to undertake the enormously important task referred to above:

> The time will come when our hands, and other parts which now seem free, will have grown solid, will have grown together with our torso, in the region of the heart. These parts will then be enclosed by a covering or membrane, just as our brain is now enclosed by the cerebral cortex and skull. That will be in the Jupiter time. The aspects for which our hands are the visible expression are in the process of becoming an organ of thinking. At the moment this is still only very rudimentary – this organ is still tiny and undeveloped. Rather as if we had only a little bump on our forehead instead of the dome of our skull, so our shoulder blades now occupy the region which will one day enclose our future brain. And you visualize the shoulder blades correctly when you regard them as little bumps of bone which really belong to a skull enclosing them, except that it is not formed yet. So you see, there is a second human being enclosed within the first.[9]

This is how we can imagine the skull of the thinking heart-brain in the chest, and how—through the exercises described in the following section of the book—we can make this picture continually more real and alive within us.

★   ★   ★

PART TWO:
THE SIX EXERCISES

Simple exercises in thinking are a far better preparation for forming proper conceptions of Saturn, Sun and Moon evolution than are complicated and learned ideas.

Rudolf Steiner

1

Structure

The following is an overview of the way the chapters about the six exercises will be structured. The sequence given here may alter slightly from chapter to chapter.

The form used is a contained and systematic one—a framework or skeleton rather than filled-out descriptions. It is up to the reader to render them fluid once more.

Terms: Some of the designations used by Rudolf Steiner for the separate exercises are first given.

Quotations from Rudolf Steiner: I will only use passages from Steiner's written descriptions, and only those which directly relate to carrying out the exercises. Such a selection, though, is not intended to limit the content under discussion. The texts quoted will be taken from the following volumes by Steiner: *How to Know Higher Worlds; The Stages of Higher Knowledge; Occult Science—an Outline;* and *Guidance in Esoteric Training.* I will not draw upon the verbal descriptions, which were mainly given either in the earlier lectures (from about 1905 to 1908) or in the 'Esoteric Lessons'.[1]

Steiner already partially sketched out the exercises in the last chapter of *Theosophy.* But in the form found there they cannot easily be compared with the sometimes more systematic descriptions of the other works listed above. To make such a comparison would go beyond the scope of the present volume.

The exercise: The essential nature of the exercise will be summed up in a phrase.

What needs to be done: The steps and stages involved in carrying out the exercise will be described.

A typical practice: If necessary, a concrete example will be given here to clarify the method of practice.

What is important: The specific characteristics of each exercise will be emphasized here.

What should be avoided: Here attention will be drawn to potential mistakes and pitfalls.

Levels of attention: Reference will be made here to three levels upon which one should focus attention as one practises the exercise, in order to carry it out in a systematic way:

- physical level—the physical environment, objects, things, one's own body, etc.
- etheric level—activities, life circumstances, etc.
- astral level—soul moods, feelings, emotions, etc.

Practical suggestions: For every exercise suggestions will be made which have arisen from actual experience. Directions of a more general nature, such as the recommended length of practice, will be found in Part Two, Chapter 9, 'The Exercise Plan'.

Etheric streams: Here the streams will be described which can make themselves felt in the astral and etheric bodies as a result of practising the exercise. These etheric streams are vibrations flowing in a certain direction. More detailed description of this can be found in Part Two, Chapter 8, 'The Etheric Streams'.

Gesture: Each exercise has a corresponding stance or gesture, which is a physical posture connected with a particular image, thought or inner gesture. These will be described in detail in Part Three of this book.

Effect: The effects of each exercise upon the physical, etheric and astral body will be described. In the case of the last three exercises, the involvement of certain supersensible, spiritual beings will be indicated.

The relationship of polar exercises: The correlation of the last three exercises with the first three will be explained.

Spirit guides: This will only be referred to in connection with the last three exercises. The supersensible beings who are involved when we carry out these exercises will be identified and briefly described.

The significance of the expressions 'control' in connection with the first three and 'fulfilment' in connection with the last three exercises will gradually become apparent.

Some readers may be put off by the mode of description, finding it too detailed and pedantic—yet I have a particular reason for adopting such a style. In the seminars I have given, which form the basis of this book, I often found that many participants came up with questions about aspects which had already been dealt with, or which could easily have been deduced from the context.

★   ★   ★

2

The First Exercise: Control of Thinking

In the midst of what we call our thinking—
which most often just flits through us
without our real involvement, he decided

to compose and gather himself, to sink
into a freely chosen thought: anchor and root
himself within it; so that, harnessed, bound

the powers of pure thought would brace him.

Christian Morgenstern[1]

Terms: Regulation or mastery of thought processes, control of thinking, control of the world of thoughts, the soul's command of its thinking processes, learning to stop thinking in a will-o'-the-wisp kind of way, developing perfect clarity of thought, concentration.

Quotations from Rudolf Steiner:

First, we pay attention to directing the sequence of our thoughts—this is the so-called 'practice of the control of thoughts' ... When we hear an illogical thought, we should immediately allow the correct thought to pass through our mind. But if we find ourselves in what seems like an illogical environment, we should not for that reason unlovingly withdraw in order to further our development. By the same token, we should not feel the immediate urge to correct any illogicality we witness round us. Rather, we should inwardly and very quietly give the thoughts rushing at us from the outside a logical and meaningful direction. We should always strive to maintain this logical direction in our own thinking.[2]

Therein, in complete inner freedom one puts a thought in the centre of one's soul, where otherwise ideas obtrude themselves upon one from without. Then one tries to keep away all intruding thoughts and feelings and to link with the first thought only what one wills to admit as suitable. Such an exercise works beneficially upon the soul and through it also upon the body. It brings the latter into such a harmonious condition that it withdraws itself from injurious influences despite the fact that the soul is not directly acting upon it.[3]

Whoever succeeds in directing his thought, for at least five minutes daily, and for months on end, to some quite commonplace object—say, for example, a needle or a pencil—and in shutting out during those five minutes all thoughts that have no connection with the object, will have made very good progress in this direction. (A fresh object may be chosen each day, or one may be continued for several days.) [...] For when we are riveting our thought for a considerable time upon something that is entirely familiar, we may be quite sure that our thinking is in accord with reality. If we ask ourselves: What is a lead pencil made of? How are the different materials prepared? How are they put together? When were lead pencils invented? and so on, we can be more sure of our thoughts being consistent with reality than if we were to ponder the question of man's origin—or, let us say, of the meaning of life.

Simple exercises in thinking are a far better preparation for forming proper conceptions of Saturn, Sun and Moon evolution than are complicated and learned ideas. As to our thinking, what is important at this stage is not the object or event to which it is directed, but that it should be strong and vigorous and to the point. If it has been educated to be so in reference to simple realities that lie open to view, it will acquire the tendency to be so even when it finds itself no longer under the control of the physical world and its laws. The pupil will find he gets rid in this way of any tendency he had before to loose and extravagant thinking.[4]

The first condition is the cultivation of absolutely clear thinking. For this purpose we must rid ourselves of the will-o'-the-wisps of thought, even if only for a very short time during the day—about five minutes (the longer, the better). We must become the rulers of our world of thought ... Therefore during this brief period, acting entirely out of our own free will, we must empty the soul of the ordinary, everyday course of events and by our own initiative place one single thought at the centre of our soul. The thought need not be a particularly striking or interesting one. Indeed it will be all the better for what has to be attained in an occult respect if a thoroughly uninteresting and insignificant thought is chosen. Thinking is then impelled to act out of its own energy, the essential thing here, whereas an interesting thought carries the thinking along with it. It is better if this exercise in thought control is undertaken with a pin rather than with Napoleon. The pupil says to himself: Now I start from this thought, and through my own inner initiative I associate with it everything that is pertinent to it. At the end of the period the thought should be just as colourful and living as it was at the beginning.[5]

The exercise: To think thoroughly and in a harmoniously structured way upon a certain object.

What needs to be done: Choose a simple, artificial (man-made) object—such as a pin, a pencil, a match, a chair or a handkerchief. Find out everything you can about it, and perhaps write this down so as to remember it well. Encyclopaedias or works on specific objects may be of use for this.[6]

Or one can familiarize oneself with the whole sequence of a production process, from the raw material to the finished product, so that a written description of this process would not be out of place in an encyclopaedia. (Rudolf Steiner himself wrote several encyclopaedia entries for the *Pierer Lexikon*.)

- Always remain factual and objective, keeping the object itself in close view and avoiding a particular slant or interpretation.
- Try hard to build up a well-structured sequence of thoughts through three, four or seven stages or levels (see below). Rather than immediately attempting the full seven stages, one can limit oneself, at least to begin with, to the first three or four.
- Once you have managed to think a sequence through correctly, it is good to picture the whole process vividly, like a film, and also to try to run it backwards.

What should be avoided:

- Thinking in an undisciplined, haphazard way

- Thinking in an associative, arbitrary, subjective, 'clever' or 'shrewd' kind of way
- Just allowing thoughts to come—in other words, drifting along passively in the thought-stream instead of being actively involved in the structuring of a sequence
- Dreaming off and losing the thread

What is important: To develop the habit of structuring organic processes of thought in such a way that they become inner necessity.

The framework of thought levels:

	external aspect (object)/inner aspect (concept)	
4. *'I'-level:*	nature, inventor	
3. *Astral level:*	design, fulfilment	necessity, usefulness
2. *Etheric level:*	production, process	origin, history
1. *Physical level:*	form and material	varying types

Questions to ask about the object:

1. What are the forms, the components, the raw materials?
2. How were the parts prepared and put together?
3. Why and for what purpose was the object designed in this way? What are my feelings about it?
4. Who invented it? When? Where?
5. Why and for what purpose did the inventor think of it?
6. How did this kind of object develop; what forerunners preceded it?
7. What are the various different types of this object—varying in form, material, use, etc.?

A typical practice: the pencil exercise

1. *Physical level (outer):* **components, form and material**
   —all that can be perceived with the five senses

   - shape, size, colour, parts
   - weight, surface texture, structure, consistency, temperature
   - tone, density
   - type of odour and its intensity (e.g. cedar wood and synthetic material)
   - taste
   - material of the different components: wood, graphite and clay (in the lead), glue, varnish and printing ink (in the wooden shaft and the writing on it), rubber and brass fitting at the top.

2. *Etheric level (outer):* **processes in time, activities** (first in the separate parts, then in their combination)

   - **wood:** forest, cutting the trees, transport (as for everything which follows), sawing up, etc.
   - **graphite mine**—graphite and clay, mining, pulverization, mixing, compacting, firing in the oven, etc.
   - **glue:** raw materials, manufacture
   - **varnish and printing ink**—extraction of oil and pigments, processing
   - **rubber**—raw materials of oil or latex, manufacture
   - **brass fitting**—mining, smelting, processing

   Then one should think about the combining of all these materials in the factory, the packing of the finished pencils, their transportation to the shops, etc.

3. *Astral level (outer):* **design, feelings**

- **design**—function, ergonomics, economic considerations
- **feelings**—qualities, suitability, aesthetic aspects, use

4. *'I'-level:* **nature, inventor**

   Who invented the pencil? Why and where and how? (Nicholas Jacques Conté invented the graphite/clay mixture in 1795, and created a pencil with it which has been hardly altered since then.)

5. *Astral level (inner):* **need for the invention, purpose and significance, consequences for daily life and for general culture, etc.**

   Great advantages over the kinds of writing instruments available at the time of its invention (the Age of Enlightenment); it therefore facilitated a new stage in cultural development (the Industrial Revolution).

6. *Etheric level (inner):* **history of the development of writing instruments, effects upon cultural evolution**

   - **sequence**—fingers, twigs, stones, brushes, stylus, slate pencils, chalk, quills, fountain-pens, mechanical pencils
   - **effects**—aided the industrial revolution by enabling thoughts to be written down quickly and easily

7. *Physical level (inner):* **the concept 'pencil' and its various forms as physical, concrete objects**

   - according to function—writing, drawing, marking etc.
   - according to size—carpenter's pencil, artist's pencil, display pencil, pocket-diary pencil, etc.

- according to shape—cylindrical, three, four, six-sided, etc.
- according to hardness:—14 different grades of hardness in total—(from 9H to 6B)

These seven stages ultimately bring the pupil to a 'pencil concept' that contains all possible kinds of pencil, including potential future ones. An archetypal image of the pencil arises as a result, the '*Ur*-pencil' if you like. Thus one proceeds from the idea of a single object to its archetypal form.

Once one has traced the complete genesis of an individual object, the direction of the exercise can be reversed—one can proceed instead from the archetype to the concrete object. The separate steps then take place in reverse order:

1. 'pencil' archetype;
2. the 'family tree' of the pencil;
3. the need for its invention (cause) and its purpose;
4. the birth of the concept in the inventor's mind;
5. design, planning and qualitative aspects;
6. manufacture and sale;
7. perceiving and picturing an actual pencil.

'I'-level	4. Inventor	
Astral level	5. Design	3. Need
Etheric level	6. Manufacture	2. Family tree
Physical level	7. Pencil	1. Archetypal pencil

This kind of sequence is related to the universal way in which material things arise from spiritual archetypes:

1. Archetype—
2. Descent through the 'family tree'—
3. The dawning intention and discovery (as conception), motivation for its creation—
4. Creation—
5. 'Embryo stage'—
6. Birth and growth—
7. Maturing, perfection/completion.

In other words, seven stages of descent.

Practical suggestions: It is a good idea to carry out the exercise early in the morning, or at least before midday. This is because it makes you wide awake and fills you with strength and energy, with 'uprightness', even when done imperfectly.

It is also good to begin with—that is, during the first cycles of repetition of all six exercises—to practise with several different objects. Then, eventually, concentrate on just one (see also the 'remarks' below).

If it should prove impossible to consider *all* the details involved—which will be true particularly of the second step, the etheric level—then one should just create additional details to allow the exercise to progress in a flowing and consecutive way. However, this imagining should be avoided as much as possible, for it is of utmost importance that the exercise be based on concrete, real facts.

Remarks: When one starts to carry out the exercise in reverse, thinking backwards through the sequence, then a rhythmic, pendulum-like *thought-wave* can arise. This exercising of our 'control of thoughts' then gives us an experience of thinking as oscillation, as wave; it manifests as an activity of and with the etheric body.

The point of the exercise, as it has so far been described, is *not* to gain mastery of the process involved but only to prepare the ground for the real esoteric process. Up to this point, the exercise can be carried out by means of our normal, intellectual thinking. The *real* exercise only begins when one has repeated it so many times and developed such good command of it that it becomes thoroughly *boring*. Not until the exercise can proceed almost by itself and automatically, until it has grown to be habit and therefore a capacity of soul, will it become possible for us to direct our whole concentration and awareness away from the object itself to the wavelike vibrations and motions of the thinking etheric body, thus concentrating upon the pure activity of thought itself. That is the real point of the exercise: experiencing the *inner* life-force. When we can experience the nature of thinking in this way, the etheric stream corresponding to such thinking will also become perceptible to us. This is also true of the other exercises.

Etheric stream: An inner *feeling* of certainty and safety, but as though carried upon rhythmically flowing water; one should pour this feeling from the forehead over the back of the head, and down into the middle of the back.

Gesture: The first position of 'I think speech':[7] periphery and centre, the world.

Effect: The capacity for thought becomes greatly strengthened. An organic, truly human quality of order either arises or is enhanced, as is the physical framework of the ego, in such a way that daily life can be more harmoniously structured.

3

The Second Exercise: Control of Will

And as the wings of thinking freed themselves,
he started to unleash his will
that all too long had languished under its yoke:

intentionally, through self-given deeds
at certain moments interrupting, lifting
it free of the round of daily tasks—

so that strength ran in streams from heart to head.

Christian Morgenstern

Terms: Control of will, control of one's actions, mastery of one's will impulses, taking the initiative, exercising the will, the soul's mastery of its will.

Quotations from Rudolf Steiner:

Second, we must bring an equally logical consistency into our actions—this is the practice of the control of actions. Any instability and disharmony in our actions injures the development of the twelve-petalled lotus flower. Therefore each of our actions should follow logically from whatever action came before. If we act today out of different principles than we did yesterday, we shall never develop the lotus flower in question.[1]

Control of actions consists of a similar regulation of these through inner freedom. A good beginning is made when one sets oneself to do regularly something that it would not have occurred to us to do in ordinary life. For in the latter, man is indeed driven to his actions from without. But the smallest action undertaken on one's innermost initiative accomplishes more in the direction indicated than all the pressures of outer life.[2]

A good exercise for the will is, every day for months on end, to give oneself the command: Today you are to do *this*, at this particular hour. One will gradually manage to fix the hour and the nature of the task so as to render the command perfectly possible to carry out.[3]

We try to think of some action which in the ordinary course of life we should certainly not have performed. Then we make it a duty to perform this action every day. It will therefore be good to choose an action which can be performed every day over as long a period of time as possible. Again it is better to begin with some insignificant action which we have to force ourselves to perform, for example, to water at a fixed time every day a pot-plant we have bought. After a certain time a second, similar act should be added to the first; later, a third, and so on . . . as many as are compatible with the carrying out of all other duties.[4]

The exercise: Every day at a certain time, command yourself to carry out an action which has no particular point or purpose for your daily activities.

What needs to be done:

- Decide upon one or several actions, and determine exactly (to the minute) when each action should be carried out. Think of a simple, insignificant action, which you would not otherwise do, and which bears absolutely no relation to daily life.

- Carry out the actions at the times decided upon, and see whether you have kept to the exact moment you intended.
- If you do not keep to the precise moment you intended, decide immediately on another time and place to carry out the action. However, do not continue trying to keep your 'appointment' more than three times in a row.
- Choose very simple actions that can be carried out in all sorts of circumstances. For example: bringing the ring finger of the left hand up to your nose, adjusting your tie, touching a shirt or blouse button, tapping your left hand three times on your right knee, ruffling your hair with your hand or describing a circle in the air with your index finger.
- Always look at the clock *after* you have carried out the action, not before!

What should be avoided:

- All usual, routine, necessary actions, such as brushing your teeth, cleaning the sink and emptying the waste-paper basket.
- All moments in the day which are connected with daily routine, such as waking up, meal-times, finishing of office hours, etc.
- Always choosing the same time or the same action; for several identical actions are really only one and the same.

What is important: This exercise can strengthen the will and help to overcome dissatisfaction and restlessness. But one can only achieve what lies within one's capacities.

Stability and inner fulfilment are dependent on striving to attain only what is within the bounds of possibility.

A typical practice:

Precondition: Having a watch with you.

1. The decision: Each day, before breakfast, I will give myself the commands for the day ahead—that is, I will choose certain actions and times when they are to be performed.

2. The command: Firstly, at 10.45, I will draw a triangle in the air with my left index finger. Second, at 14.00, I will stand up and breathe deeply three times. Third, at 16.42 . . .

3. Frequency: Three to five actions per day. More is unrealistic, at least to begin with, because of the necessary repetitions caused by missing the right moment.

4. Failure: If the right moment is missed, then you should immediately, on the spot, choose a new time when the action will be repeated. It is advisable to avoid similar times, i.e. if you have missed carrying out an action at 11.30 it is better not to choose 12.30 or 16.30, but 12.53 or 16.22.

The outer *aim* is to gain such mastery that you can set your watch by your own newly developed sense of time, and be correct to the minute.

Levels of attention: you will soon notice that you do not have equal success in carrying out your intentions in all situations and at all times. It can be helpful, therefore, to direct your attention to the circumstances which present the greatest hindrance, or under which the action is easier to perform. These circumstances can relate to various different levels, and depend, perhaps, on the following things:

On the physical level: whether you are dealing with concrete objects, during physical labour for example; whether you are in an open or enclosed space; whether the action is focused upon your own body or not, etc.

On the etheric level: whether the action is to be carried out during an active or quiet period in the day, while you are engaged in mental or practical work, during work time or free time; whether you are feeling ill or well, etc.

On the astral level: whether you are in a better or worse frame of mind; whether the situation you are engaged in requires great concentration, e.g. at conferences, during conversations, during business meetings, while writing, driving, etc; whether you are relaxed, playing music, having a lunch break, on holiday, etc.

Practical suggestions: At the very beginning it is better not to undertake more than two actions per day, so as to have enough time to allow for the repetitions necessitated by missing the right moment.

If you notice that you cannot remember the commands, it is helpful to write them down somewhere, for example in your pocket diary, until this becomes no longer necessary.

Etheric stream: A feeling of initiative and energy, like a stream of rushing water passing from the head down over the forehead to the heart, and flowing on into the whole upper portion of the body.

Gesture: The second position of 'I think speech'. From the centre to the periphery. I (work) into the world.

The effect: By bringing this exercise to a certain degree of perfection, one frees oneself more and more from the tyranny of time, thereby *creating* time in the process. One learns mastery over one's own will impulses, thus taking control of the activity of the etheric body, which is one's own time-body. The capacity for willing takes root in a new foundation, and is no longer sucked continually into the onward rush of time.

There is in fact a difference between this ever onward, ongoing flow of chronological time, to which we are subject, and the kind of time which is 'right' for our destiny. The ancient Greeks had two terms for 'time': the one, which was measurable, physical, chronological time they called *chronos*; and the other, the immeasurable, qualitative, right time, they called *kairos*. (The time connected in the Gospels with the life and deeds of Christ is always *kairos*, and is therefore never subject to the laws of physical time.) We can all experience the elasticity of time, the way it often does not seem to correspond to measurable clock-time. Sometimes it contracts to an unbelievably short instant, sometimes it stretches out unbearably.

The real aim of this exercise, then, is to overcome the tyranny of time and to find for oneself the *kairos* of one's own destiny, the 'right' moment. Once this aim has been attained, one becomes able to create time for oneself. Then one no longer needs to say, 'I don't have time,' but, 'I have time because I will it (I create it).'

4

The Third Exercise: Control of Feeling

So long as we fail to find composure, calm
through every stroke of fortune—glad or sad,
so long we'll fail to grasp the world.

Leave love, leave hate aside; we must
seek the deeper sense of pain and joy.
Then only will the senses' veil part—

then only can God speak His word to us.

Christian Morgenstern

Terms: Equanimity, achieving balance in life, bearing patiently, balance (emotional), inner composure, the soul's mastery over its feelings, rising above joy and sorrow, overcoming likes and dislikes.

In some places, the *sixth* exercise is described as 'inner soul balance',[1] 'inner balance',[2] and 'balance'.[3]

In one single passage, in the book *How to Know Higher Worlds*, this exercise does not figure as the third but as the *sixth;* its position in the sequence is therefore different from that given in all other descriptions. Various inner reasons, which will become clear in the course of what follows, show that it really is the third exercise.

This need not cause us too much confusion if we recall the 'uncertainty principle' mentioned in Part One, Chapter 1.

Quotations from Rudolf Steiner:

Sixth, we must achieve a certain balance in life (or serenity). As esoteric students, we should strive to maintain a mood of inner harmony whether joy or sorrow comes to meet us. We should lose the habit of swinging between being 'up one minute and down the next'. Instead we should be as prepared to deal with misfortune and danger as with joy and good fortune.[4]

Endurance consists in holding oneself at a distance from moods which continually vascillate between being 'over the moon' and 'down in the dumps'. Man is driven to and fro among all kinds of moods. Pleasure makes him glad; pain depresses him. This has its justification. But he who seeks the path to higher knowledge must be able to mitigate joy and also grief. He must become stable. He must with moderation surrender to pleasurable impressions and also painful experiences; he must move with dignity through both. He must never be unmanned nor disconcerted. This does not produce lack of feeling, but it brings man to the steady centre within the ebbing and flowing tide of life around him. He has himself always in hand.[5]

Passing on now to the world of feeling, the pupil must succeed in reaching a certain equanimity of soul. For this he will need to have under his control all outward expression of pleasure or pain, of joy or sorrow. Such advice will be certain to meet with prejudice. Surely, if he is not to rejoice over what is joyful, not to sorrow over what is sorrowful, the pupil will become utterly indifferent to the life that is going on around him! But this is not at all what is meant. The pupil shall by all means rejoice over what is joyful and sorrow over what is sorrowful. It is the outward expression of joy and sorrow, of pleasure and pain that he must learn to control. If he honestly tries to attain this, he will soon discover that he does not grow less but actually more sensitive than before to everything in his environment that can arouse emotions of joy or of pain. If the pupil is really to succeed in cultivating this control it will undoubtedly involve keeping close watch upon himself for a long time. He must not be slow to enter with fullness of feeling into pleasure and pain, but he must be able to do so without losing self-control and giving involuntary expression to it. What he has to suppress is not the pain—*that* is justified—but the involuntary weeping; not the horror at a base action, but the outburst of blind fury; not the caution in face of danger, but the giving way to panic—which does no good whatever.[6]

In the third month, life should be centred on a new exercise—the development of a certain equanimity towards the fluctuations of joy and sorrow, pleasure and pain; 'heights of jubilation' and 'depths of despair' should quite consciously be replaced by an equable mood. Care is taken that no pleasure shall carry us away, no sorrow plunge us into the depths, no experience lead to immoderate fear or vexation, no expectation give rise to anxiety or fear, no situation disconcert us, and so on.[7]

The exercise: Learning to master the *expression* of your own feelings so completely that only those are expressed *outwardly* which you yourself determine, or none at all.

A typical practice:

Preparatory exercise: First strive to become quite familiar with your own feelings, particularly the way these are expressed in your face. For this purpose, find a peaceful period of at least 15 minutes each day, and dwell as thoroughly as possible upon the usual expressions of your feeling-life. Only then should you begin with the exercise proper. It will often be too difficult to trace immediately *all* your feeling impulses and the way they are expressed; so you can just practise the exercise for a while with what you have discovered, and then extend it to explore further kinds of feeling and their outward form.

This exercise takes place in three stages spread over two days:

In a *first* step, during a quiet period of at least 15 minutes, choose a few expressions of emotion, ones that you know belong to your daily 'repertoire', and undertake to change these during the next day: to moderate them if they are too overbearing; to bring them more strongly to expression if they are too weak or do not appear at all on your face or 'body language'. The idea is to arrive at a balanced, middle level of expression. Once you have mastered these manifestations of emotion to a great enough extent, you can decide to prevent them finding expression at all.

In a *second* step, you can try, during the next day, to put into effect what you have undertaken to do, that is, changing the modes of expression of various feelings, *though not the feelings themselves.*

The *third* step involves first reviewing, in the daily quiet period, what you have practised, and then in the light of this review deciding on the course your practice should take the following day.

So you structure this exercise in such a way that the first

and third parts of it take place in the daily quiet period—the
first part on one day, the second on the following—while
the second part is practised throughout the whole day.

What needs to be done:

- To prepare this exercise you will need to draw up a list
  of your own expressions of feeling—without at first
  relating them to each other in any way. Things which
  might, for example, appear on this list are: sharp words,
  angry looks, impatient gestures and words, grimaces,
  raised voice, cold or damp or shaking hands, blushing,
  tears, being lost for words, swearing, grumbling or
  moaning, chattering away uncontrollably, sighing, a red
  face, explosive laughter, stomach ache—all of which are
  involuntary. Then you can start to distinguish between
  the forms of expression, which are more 'inner' from
  those which are more 'outward'. The list can be
  extended with feelings themselves: sorrow and joy,
  pleasure and suffering, despondency and exuberance,
  recklessness and courage, sympathy and hatred, etc.
- Since we do not usually notice all our own expressions
  of feeling, you can ask good friends to draw them to
  your attention, and describe them, acting as a kind of
  mirror.
- Notice especially how and in what way you exaggerate
  your own expressions of feeling. In the same way, if you
  see that certain expressions are held back and subdued,
  try to practise reinvigorating them.
- It is vital to observe yourself with scrupulous, unsparing
  honesty.

The *aim* of this exercise is to develop a rich, fluid,
unhampered feeling life, and at the same time to become

master of its heights and depths—in other words, you learn to occupy the middle ground in which expressions of sympathy and antipathy balance each other, and in whose free space your feeling life can live most intensely. For you can only have a broad, harmonious register of feelings when they are not limited by a lack of expressive possibilities.

What should be avoided:

- Justifying and excusing your own expressions of feeling—rationalizing, in other words.
- Deceiving yourself through dishonest self-observation, deluding yourself.
- Rejecting the help of others, because you want to find out for yourself how you express things.
- Repressing the feelings themselves instead of their expression.

Determining factors: the temperaments are important factors in the expression of your feeling life, considerably influencing exaggeration or repression. Being aware of your own temperament makes it easier to discover the best mode of practice.

Cholerics and *sanguines* should practise limiting the expression of their feelings.

Phlegmatics and *melancholics* should try consciously to enhance and intensify their emotional expression. It is better, though, to find ways of matching them to particular circumstances, and even if this is not possible at first, still to experiment with doing so.

Levels of attention: The above list of types of emotional expression can be structured more systematically by taking account of the following three levels:

Physical level: chiefly the facial expressions and body language (gestures, positions), but also the expressions which are harder to control, such as blushing, tears, shaking, coldness, sweating, etc.

Etheric level: attention should, on the one hand, be focused on outer gesture (running away in panic, crying, laughing uproariously, etc), and, on the other hand, on more psychosomatic reactions such as stomach- and headache, depressive or hysterical reactions, etc.

Astral level: this is mostly connected with one's own emotional states: excitement, coldness, indifference, being distant and reserved, despondency, embarassment, shame, etc.

What is important: To develop a *rich* feeling life, without however being compelled to any involuntary show of emotion—feeling without compulsively expressing it.

Practical suggestions: It can be helpful to imagine the different feelings in terms of colour and form, and also to try to draw or paint them. This helps to grasp them in a much more concrete kind of way, and to influence them more easily.

A particularly effective way of gauging your degree of success is to mark your failures each day, not your achievements, on a pocket diary—one which shows a whole month on one sheet—with a black dot (see Fig. 10). As you continue to practise the exercise, the sheets will gradually grow less dark from month to month, allowing you to recognize your success. That can give new courage!

It is not necessary to take account of every single mode of expression that you have. It is a better idea to select two to four kinds of gesture/expression, and when you achieve some success with one of these to increase them to three to five.

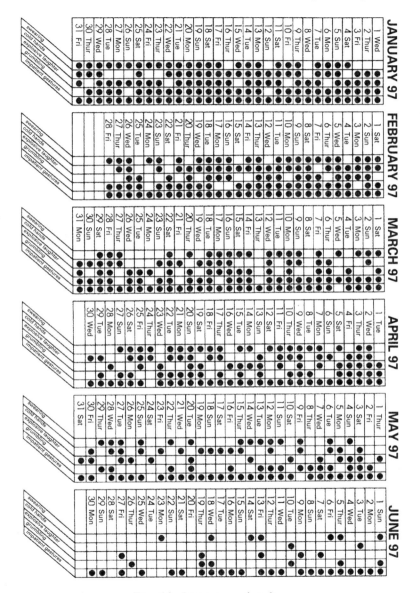

Fig. 10: List in a pocket diary

Etheric stream: A feeling of peace, inner warmth and joyful tranquillity, concentrated in the heart and from there flowing into the hands, then to the feet and lastly back to the head. An awareness that your own, mastered feeling life is anchored in the earth through your feet, that it radiates out through the hands into your own actions, and through the head illuminates your own intentions.

Gesture: The third position of 'I think speech'. The star-human. Spirit in me.

Effect: By attaining independence, composure, inner stability and sovereignty, in other words by mastering the astral body, the latter becomes a source of soul warmth and light. Feeling finds a new foundation, liberating itself from the compulsion to express itself in involuntary ways.

5

The Fourth Exercise:
The Fulfilment of Thinking in Feeling

Beside a corpse—a foully rotting dog—
Master Jesus slows his steps and stops
unlike his distressed disciples hurrying past.

Why stop? the murmur rises from their midst:
Is it bad faith to feel sick at the sight?
But then, ashamed, they hear their master speak

praises of the animal's white teeth.

Christian Morgenstern

Terms: Tolerance, patience, trust in your surroundings, attitude of affirmation, positivity, open-mindedness and impartiality, seeing the true and the beautiful in all things.

This exercise is only referred to as freedom from bias on one single occasion: 'The fourth exercise can be called "freedom from bias".'[1] Elsewhere, this term is used in connection with the fifth exercise. Once again, the 'uncertainty principle' applies, as explained in Part One, Chapter 1.

Quotations from Rudolf Steiner:

Fourth, we must develop forbearance (or tolerance) towards other people, other beings, and events. We must suppress all unnecessary criticism of imperfection, evil and wickedness and seek rather to understand everything that comes to meet us. Just as the sun does not withdraw its light from wickedness and evil, so we, too, should not withdraw our understanding and sympathy from anyone. When we meet adversity, we should not indulge in negative judgements but accept the inevitable and try, as best we can, to turn it to the good. Similarly, instead of considering the opinions of others only from our own standpoint, we should try to put ourselves into their position.[2]

Another important quality is the 'yea saying' sense. This can be developed in one who in all things has an eye for the good, beautiful and purposeful aspects of life, and not, primarily, for the blameworthy, ugly and contradictory.[3]

It will be a further help to the education of his thinking and feeling if the pupil acquire a virtue that I will call positiveness [...] The spurious, the bad and the ugly should not hinder us from finding, wherever they are present, the true, the good and the beautiful. Positiveness must not be confused with lack of discrimination, or with an arbitrary shutting of one's eyes to what is bad, or false, or 'good for nothing'.[4]

In the fourth month, as a new exercise, what is sometimes called a 'positive attitude' to life should be cultivated. It consists in seeking always for the good, the praiseworthy, the beautiful and the like, in all beings, all experiences, all things [...] [The esoteric pupil] will soon notice that under the veil of something repugnant there is a hidden beauty, that even under the outer guise of a criminal there is a hidden good, that under the mask of a lunatic the divine soul is somehow concealed.

In a certain respect this exercise is connected with what is called 'abstention from criticism'. This is not to be understood in the sense of calling black white and white black. There is, however, a difference between a judgement which, proceeding merely from one's own personality, is coloured with the element of personal sympathy or antipathy, and an attitude which enters lovingly into the alien phenomenon or being, always asking: How has it come to be like this or to act like this? Such an attitude will by its very nature be more set upon helping what is imperfect than upon simply finding fault and criticizing.

The objection that the very circumstances of their lives oblige many people to find fault and condemn is not valid here. For in such cases the circumstances are such that the person in question cannot go through a genuine occult training. There are indeed many circumstances in life which make occult schooling impossible, beyond a certain point. In such a case the person should not impatiently desire, in spite of everything, to make progress which is possible only under some conditions.[5]

The exercise: To find the positive aspects of everything which happens to you or which you encounter.

What needs to be done:

- Whenever you encounter something, some situation, a thought, a person or a creature which makes a negative, unpleasant or repulsive impression on you, you should try to see its positive aspects.
- You should select a few particular perceptions that arise in your daily life, and, at the very moment you observe

them, find at least *one* positive aspect of each, think at least *one* positive thought about each one. It is true wisdom to realize that no one is ever wholly in the right, nor wholly in the wrong. It will therefore be possible to find something positive in *every* situation.

- The positive aspect should be sought within the perceived object/person, situation, etc. itself.
- Once you have perceived the positive aspect, and made yourself fully conscious of it, you should cultivate within yourself the feelings that belong to it.
- Confine yourself to seeking only the positive aspect.
- Become aware of your own constitutional tendency to perceive negative aspects far more easily and quickly than positive ones—as though the negative had the power to drown out and conceal the positive.

What should be avoided:

- Forming 'positive' ideas in an intentional, exaggerated and subjective manner, instead of finding the real positive qualities within the object/person, etc.
- Intentionally cultivating sympathetic feelings which are not founded upon clear and concrete observations.
- Finding something positive later on, instead of during the actual process of observation.
- Turning this exclusive focus on the positive into a general attitude towards life, so that your healthy sense of judgement is impaired.

What is important:

- Remembering that this exercise is, as a spiritual exercise, only of value at the moment you practise it.
- Not losing your capacity for clear judgement.

● Becoming aware that the soul has a strong natural tendency to negativity, and controlling this tendency.

A 'prime example':

The following Persian legend about Jesus Christ, which Rudolf Steiner related several times, not only sums up the essence of this exercise but also points to the source from which positivity flows. I will cite the versions from *The Stages of Higher Knowledge*, and from the passage in *Guidance in Esoteric Training* which directly refers to it:

> In Persian poetry there is a beautiful legend about Christ, which illustrates the meaning of this quality. A dead dog is lying on the road. Among the passersby is Christ. All the others turn away from the ugly sight; only Christ pauses and speaks admiringly of the animal's beautiful teeth. It is possible to look at things in this way, and he who earnestly seeks for it may find in all things, even the most repulsive, something worthy of acknowledgement. The fruitfulness in things is not in what is lacking in them, but in what they have.[6]

> This quality of soul is best characterized by a Persian legend concerning Christ Jesus. One day, as He was walking with His disciples, they saw a dead dog lying by the roadside in a state of advanced decomposition. All the disciples turned away from the disgusting sight; Christ Jesus alone did not move but looked thoughtfully at the corpse and said: 'What beautiful teeth the animal has!' Where the others had seen only the repulsive, the unpleasant, he looked for the beautiful. So must the esoteric pupil strive to seek for the positive in every phenomenon and in every being.[7]

Levels of attention:

The wealth of things and beings which allow this exercise to unfold can be distinguished according to the same three levels already mentioned:

Physical level: physical objects of all kinds, such as stones, artificial (man-made) objects, but also the living bodies of plants, animals and people.

Etheric level: phenomena suited to this exercise are, on the one hand, natural occurrences such as storms, tempests, earthquakes and floods; and on the other, phenomena of social interaction—although one must be very careful in this realm. The positive aspects of such things as a marriage break-up, an illness, even a crime, can usually only be recognized after we have gained some distance from it through the passage of time. It is therefore often better just to keep an open mind on the positive potential of such events and withhold judgement.

Astral level: views and opinions, (philosophical) world-views, ideas etc.—all things which can easily be laughed out of court and dismissed if they do not coincide with our own conceptions.

Another systematic kind of ordering could make use of the categories: good, beautiful, true.

Practical suggestions: It can be very helpful to write down the phenomena and occurrences which you know you feel antipathy towards. This list can then be expanded through further observation. You may be astonished to find how many phenomena, statements, situations there are that you suddenly realize you react negatively to.

Etheric stream: A feeling of blessedness and great joy, as though you are expanding. This is concentrated in the heart to begin with; then, and chiefly, radiates out through the eyes into your surroundings; then also through the ears and the whole surface of the skin. You will experience yourself as outspread etheric body—love as an active force of feeling.

Gesture: The fourth position of 'I think speech'. Centre and periphery. I in spirit.

Effect: The fourth exercise helps us overcome the adversarial force of Lucifer. It frees the astral body from Lucifer's negativity (primal lie and illusion), perfects the capacity for thinking and feeling, and strengthens the soul in its effort to gain control and sovereignty of itself. Feelings are liberated from a constricting entanglement in the either/or of sympathy and antipathy.

*

Some explanation is needed at this point. What follows here is also relevant for the corresponding sections in the next exercises.

Three supersensible, spiritual forces or beings, called in anthroposophy *Lucifer, Ahriman* and the *Asuras* (Asura in the singular), have an effect upon the evolution of the various bodies of the human being: Lucifer affects the astral body, Ahriman the etheric body and the Asuras the physical body. In contrast to the long-apparent influences of Lucifer and Ahriman, the effect of the Asuras has only started to be perceptible since the beginning of this century. The 'nature of evil' which first manifested through Lucifer, then through Ahriman, has now begun to culminate and reach its broadest dimensions through the Asuras.

People do not normally differentiate between various evil beings. They lump them all together as the devil, Satan, evil, the adversary, etc. But anthroposophy does make clear distinctions between the three powers mentioned here. These beings have received the task of opposing the human being, in order that he may develop and evolve. It is therefore *essential* nowadays—although this may require an enormous effort—carefully to distinguish the characteristic effects of the Asuras from those of luciferic and, particularly, ahrimanic beings. It is only by so doing that one can become aware at all of the Asuras' existence, and confront them with courage and steadfastness. If we do not do this, the Asuras will, now and in the future, remain concealed and unrecognized, shielding themselves behind the ahrimanic beings, thereby continually intensifying their influence. The tragic consequence of this will be that human beings will not be able to pursue their proper path of evolution. The effects of the Asuras can be seen in several phenomena of recent times: homeless people, senseless murders (people who run amok), rape, perverse sexuality, feelings of life's pointlessness, terrorism for the sake of it, chaos—in politics and the economy in particular—illnesses of the auto-immune system (Aids, immune system weaknesses), etc.

The human body is the physical expression of our thinking ego-being; and thinking on the physical level is the foundation of our human nature. The Asuras specifically attack this thinking. By immersing our thinking activity, through the physical senses, in the sense world, thoughts arise in us of a lower, sensual, emotional, self-involved kind.

When we think self-involved thoughts, these beings are delighted. In other respects they are more developed and advanced than human beings, but they have a desire to be embodied in the astral forms which we ourselves create. These beings are the ones known as the Asuras. Whenever we think in lower thought forms, we provide them with nourishment.[8]

Our present-day, normal, logical thinking carries within it the tendency to produce ever more rigid and dead thought-forms. Against this we must now set a higher, new, living thinking, so that the Asuras begin to 'starve' and so that we will be able to overpower them in the future. (In this connection see Part Four: 'The New Heart-Thinking'.)

Exercising positivity creates a counterbalance to the primal negativity and its effects which Lucifer has woven into the astral body.

But fully in keeping with this positivity, we can recognize a positive—since necessary—effect of these beings and their influence. They are the spiritual beings who provide us with the opposition needed to develop our own particular powers and capacities, so that we can fulfil our own individual destiny as well as that of humanity in general. In this sense, human life is in itself a 'training'; and Lucifer, Ahriman and the Asuras are the ones who train us as we pass through life. Behind their masks as 'adversaries', therefore, we can see them as being of enormous help to human beings.

The relationship of the fourth exercise to the third: The fourth exercise has also been called 'the exercise for thinking and feeling'. It allows the astral body (perceiving or feeling body), which was harmed by 'The Fall' or 'Original Sin', to unite the strengthened thinking of the first exercise with feeling. This cleanses and transforms our emotional life.

Our human feelings as they are today, our whole emotional life, has arisen through Lucifer's effect upon the astral body. The astral body was bound to the sense world through the 'temptation' of Lucifer—the Serpent of the paradisaical Tree of Knowledge—and we are dependent upon this world in our feelings. This is the astral body aspect of 'Original Sin'.

The third exercise relates to the inner aspect of the luciferic temptation, the fourth to the outer aspect; a polarity arises between them: in the third exercise our perception is focused directly upon ourselves, while in the fourth it is directed towards the world.

Spirit guides: The Spirits of Will (Thrones). They cleanse the astral body of Original Sin, restoring the original nature of the will.

The three 'trainers', Lucifer, Ahriman and the Asuras, are the chief providers of the opposition which human beings need in order to develop and transform their three bodies (physical, etheric and astral). There are, however, three far mightier spiritual beings who counteract them, and who act as guides and helpers of humanity, ensuring that Lucifer, Ahriman and the Asuras remain within the bounds of their task. These powerful beings (the Hierarchies) belong to the highest being-levels of the universe, and protect the human being's three bodies:

The Spirits of Will (Thrones) protect the astral body.
The Spirits of Harmony (Cherubim) protect the etheric body.
The Spirits of Love (Seraphim) protect the physical body.

By working through the fourth exercise at the transformation of the damaged astral body, the Thrones simultaneously enhance in us the power of will. The Spirits of

Will have allowed Lucifer to implant a 'bad will' into the astral body. This brought about the dimming of our perceptions of the world of spirit, on the one hand, and on the other a *non-perceiving* of what is good, beautiful and true in the sense world—a primal negativity in the astral body. The fourth exercise enables the astral body gradually to free itself from, and be cleansed of this bad will, so that 'good will' can be reinstated instead. That is the precondition for the transformation of the astral body in the *spirit-self.*

6

The Fifth Exercise:
The Fulfilment of Thinking in the Will

Just give over with your fairy-tales!
You say the Tower of Pisa has stopped leaning?
In my world-view, wonders just don't happen.

Then your world-view's much poorer, I'm afraid.
Of course, believing every superstition's
not right; but just as surely show no mercy

to the faint heart in you which has no belief.

Christian Morgenstern

Terms: Impartiality, thinking connected to will, lack of prejudice, continual openness, faith. (The term 'faith' should be understood in relationship to the term 'impartiality' applied in the fourth exercise.)

Quotations from Rudolf Steiner:

Fifth, we must develop openness and impartiality towards all the phenomena of life. This is sometimes called faith or trust. We must learn to approach every person, every being, with trust. Such trust or confidence must inspire all our actions. We should never say, in reply to something said to us, 'I don't believe that because it contradicts the opinion I have already formed.' Rather, when faced with something new, we must always be willing to test our opinions and views and revise them if necessary. We must always remain receptive to whatever approaches us. We should trust in the effectiveness of whatever we undertake. All doubt and timidity should be banished from our being. If we have a goal, we must have faith in the power of our goal. Even a hundred failures should not be able to take this faith from us. This is the 'faith that can move mountains'.[1]

Further, it is important to develop the quality of 'impartiality'. Every human being has had his own experiences and has formed from them a fixed set of opinions according to which he directs his life. Just as conformity to experience is of course necessary, on the one hand, it is also important that he who would pass through spiritual development to higher knowledge should always keep an eye open for everything new and unfamiliar that confronts him. He will be as cautious as possible with judgements such as, 'That is impossible', 'That cannot be'. Whatever opinion he may have formed from previous experiences, he will be ready at any moment, when he encounters something new, to admit a new opinion. All love of one's own opinion must vanish.[2]

The thinking, and together with it the will, reaches a degree of maturity if one tries never to let past experiences rob one of open-minded receptivity for new ones. To declare in the face of some new experience: 'I never heard of such a thing, I don't believe it!' should make no sense at all to a pupil of the Spirit. Rather let him make the deliberate resolve, during a specific period of time, to let every thing or being he encounters tell him something new. A breath of wind, a leaf falling from a tree, the prattle of a little child, can all teach us something, are we but ready to adopt a point of view to which we have hitherto perhaps not been accustomed. One can, it is true, carry this too far. We must not, at whatever age we have reached, put right out of our minds everything we have experienced hitherto. We have most decidedly to base our judgement of what confronts us now upon past experience. That is one side of the balance, but on the other there is the need for the pupil of the Spirit to be ready all the time for entirely new experiences; above all, to admit to himself the possibility that the new may contradict the old.[3]

In the fifth month, efforts should be made to develop the feeling of confronting every new experience with complete open-mindedness. The esoteric pupil must break entirely with the attitude which, in the face of something just heard or seen, exclaims: 'I never heard that, or I never saw that, before; I don't believe it—it's an illusion.' At every moment he must be ready to encounter and accept absolutely new experiences. What he has hitherto recognized as being in accordance with natural law, or what he has regarded as possible, should present no obstacle to the acceptance of a new truth. Although radically expressed, it is absolutely correct that if anyone were to come to the esoteric pupil and say, 'Since last night the steeple of such and such a church has tilted right over,' the esotericist should leave a loophole open [to the possibility that] his previous knowledge of natural law could somehow be augmented by such an apparently unprecedented fact.[4]

The exercise: To be able to envisage that what seems impossible is not!

What needs to be done:

- Every time you encounter a thing, a statement, a situation, etc. that seems unbelievable or impossible, try to open yourself to its possibility at the very moment you encounter it.
- Depending on the circumstances, either say out loud or to yourself the following or a similar formula: 'Yes, that could be possible under certain conditions.' You can also add: 'For I haven't yet experienced everything that exists.'
- Make yourself attentive and watchful for the moments in life when this exercise can be practised.
- Become aware of your innate, constitutional tendency to believe that only what you have already experienced, what you already know, and what is familiar to you, is true and real.
- Open the soul to new possibilities. Be of an open mind to everything which you encounter.

What should be avoided:

- Waiting for a later moment before deciding what you think about it.
- Only 'going through the motions', not inwardly affirming and admitting that you, like all other people, cannot know everything there is to be known.
- Accepting something unknown without really thinking about it.
- Becoming too credulous and gullible.

What is important:

- Developing a clear picture of the imperfection and incompleteness of your own experiences.

- Not just believing, but practising openness and open-mindedness.
- Understanding the actual circumstances and conditions as clearly as possible; providing a carefully considered, rigorous basis for the inner attitude of openness.
- Becoming unprejudiced and impartial.

Levels of attention: Once again, we can allocate the experiences and phenomena involved in this exercise to three different levels. The following example given by Rudolf Steiner applies to the physical level:

> Although radically expressed, it is absolutely correct that if anyone were to come to the esoteric pupil and say, 'Since last night the steeple of such and such a church has tilted right over,' the esotericist should leave a loophole open [to the possibility that] his previous knowledge of natural law could somehow be augmented by such an apparently unprecedented fact.[5]

Physical level: Reports, and also your own experience, of unusual, 'impossible' occurrences, such as the Loch Ness monster, UFOs, extraterrestrial beings, etc. Many such reports appear in the tabloid press, but this should apply also to scientific reports.
Etheric level: Walking on water, levitation, spontaneous combustion, instant dematerialization, resurrection, etc.
Astral level: Clairvoyance, near-death experiences, channelling, New Age ideas, spirit beings (spirit guides during channelling or spirit healing), etc.

Practical suggestions: If, as with the fourth exercise, you draw up a list, you will probably become gradually more aware of the large number of things you have rejected up to now.

Etheric stream: A subtle feeling like very delicately vibrating air, which streams and pours into your body from the world around through your eyes, ears and your whole skin. You suck it into yourself. You have the feeling that you can perceive in other ways than through your physical sense organs. Love as activity.

Gesture: The fifth position of 'I think speech'. From the periphery to the centre. Spirit in me.

Effect: The fifth exercise helps overcome Ahriman. It frees the etheric body from dependency on sense impressions, and from being harnessed to the ongoing rush of time. The veil of materialistic illusion created by Ahriman is brushed aside. We can become free of the past's influence as the single determining factor of our life.

Ahriman works in the etheric, living realm of the outer world. (Lucifer, on the other hand, is active in the inner world of the soul.) Ahriman is the bearer of the power of death and dying, and oversees the flow of chronological time, of 'chronos' (whereas Lucifer rules in the stream of consciousness of the astral body). His influence also extends to the human will, in the realm of the life-forces and within the human organism. In this realm he also affects the physiology of the organs of perception, whose capacities he limits and renders less sensitive, so that they cannot penetrate beyond sense phenomena. The consequence of this is that normally we can only perceive the material world in a concrete and direct way. But when one overcomes such opposition, when, for example, one manages to exclude the sense of sight limited by Ahriman *without excluding seeing itself*, then supersensible seeing—'clairvoyance'—can arise. Clairvoyance is actually a will-process, but one in which the will is no longer bound to the sense world, but liberated from it.

The relationship of the fifth exercise to the second: The fifth exercise is active on the etheric level. In this realm the will strengthened in the second exercise now lessens its dependency on the flow of earthly, chronological time. The power of thinking achieved through the first exercise now unites in the fifth exercise with the will strengthened in the second. This enables the 'bad will', which banished us to 'ex-istence' ('ex' meaning 'out') from life within the spirit world, to transform itself gradually into 'good will'. The life of the world of spirit is then mirrored once more in human life.

Spirit guides: The Spirits of Harmony (Cherubim). They tear asunder the illusion of time in the etheric body.

The Cherubim oversee the life of the universe, the harmonious, resounding confluence of all the parts and processes of the world. They also supervise Ahriman's activity in the human etheric body. It is *chronos* or chronological time which draws us down out of world harmony, out of eternity. If we can rise above *chronos* and enter into *kairos*, then we can increasingly enable our own life to unfold in the *right time*, and reunite with eternity.

Through the fifth exercise we open ourselves to the world of spirit, brushing aside the veil of time which Ahriman has woven. To the awareness of truth attained by the fourth exercise is now added the experience of beauty.

7

The Sixth Exercise:
The Fulfilment of Thinking in Thinking

> Creature no longer, now he creates his thoughts,
> Lord, not slave now, of his will,
> measure and master of the tides of feeling,
>
> too deep to suffer injury from rejection,
> too free to give obduracy dwelling space;
> a human being unites with spirit realms:
>
> and finds the path towards the throne of thrones.
>
> *Christian Morgenstern*

This exercise is the hardest to understand and to carry out, for it is really concerned with creating an inner, pure thought-concept, and then observing and thinking it through.

Terms: Harmony, harmony of soul, steadfastness, persistence, soul-balance, inner balance, inner balance and inner harmony, harmony of the powers of spirit, harmonization of the five attributes, uniting the five exercises, unison or accord between the mind, feelings, and moral sphere, harmonious unity.

The 'balance' which has such emphasis here was a term used to describe the third exercise. It is remarkable that there are so many different terms referring to this sixth exercise, for there is less explanation of the way it is to be practised than for any of the others.

Quotations from Rudolf Steiner:

Third [sic!], we must cultivate perseverance. As long as we consider a goal we have set ourselves to be right and worthy, we should never let any outside influence deter us from striving to reach it. We should consider obstacles as challenges to be overcome, not as reasons for giving up.[1]

When the five above-mentioned qualities have been acquired, a sixth then presents itself as a matter of course: inner balance, the harmony of the spiritual forces. The human being must find within himself a spiritual centre of gravity that gives him firmness and security in the face of all that would pull him hither and thither in life. The sharing in all surrounding life must not be shunned, and everything must be allowed to work upon one. Not flight from all the distracting activities of life is the correct course, but rather, the full devoted yielding to life, *along with* the sure, firm guarding of inner balance and harmony.[2]

These then are five qualities of soul the pupil has to acquire in the course of a right and proper training: control over the direction of his thoughts, control of his impulses of will, equanimity in the face of pleasure and pain, positiveness in his attitude to the world around him, readiness to meet life with an open mind. Lastly, when he has spent consecutive periods of time in training himself for the acquisition of these five qualities, the pupil will need to bring them into harmony in his soul. He will have to practise them in manifold combinations—two by two, three and one at a time, and so on, in order to establish harmony among them.[3]

In the sixth month, endeavours should be made to repeat all the five exercises again, systematically and in regular alternation. In this way a beautiful equilibrium of soul will gradually develop.[4]

The exercise: Think carefully and thoroughly about the nature of all six exercises. By simultaneously practising the previous five, the sixth comes into existence.

What needs to be done:

- For your daily practice, choose *groups* of exercises each time, for example:
  groups of two: 1 and 2; 1 and 3, etc.; 2 and 3 etc.; 3 and 4...
  groups of three: 1 and 2 and 3; 1 and 2 and 4...
  groups of four: 1 and 2 and 3 and 4...
- Recognize and compare the similar and differing qualities of what you practise.
- Try clearly to grasp the dynamic of each exercise.
- Use the sevenfold body and soul structure of the human being as the basis for your practice, recognizing the relationship of each exercise to one of the seven levels of the human being, and practise with the relevant level as your focus.
- Relate the three soul-forces of thinking, feeling and will to the three adversarial forces of the Asuras, Lucifer, and Ahriman, and to the three bodies: physical, etheric and astral.
- Spread the chosen exercises out over the whole day. Try to see that only your own 'I' activity can give rise to and carry out the exercises; how this exercising unfolds; and that the 'I' can work through its various bodily sheaths with the help of all six exercises.

What should be avoided:

- Just practising the other exercises separately, for them-selves and not discovering (recognizing) the harmony between them all as a whole organism of exercises; this means that you haven't actually practised the sixth exercise
- Seeking intellectual, arbitrary, subjective connections and relationships, which do not arise from your actual experience of practising the exercises

A typical practice:

During each day of practice, first choose some of the other (five) exercises and practise them together, in all possible combinations: two, three, four, or all five together.

At the end of the day, but also while practising, observe the character of each exercise, comparing it with that of the others so as to find the organic connections and relation-ships between them.

Finally, try to order the individual exercises as parts of the whole *exercise organism*; then perceive, observe and think through this totality.

This holistic, integrative perspective allows us to see that these six exercises are not arbitrarily put together, but that each is part of a unified organism. Only when you have understood this total organism can you perceive the basis and purpose, and also the effect of these exercises.

The living essence of this exercise organism can be represented in the following schematic form:

(*'I'-level*)	(the active 'I')	
Astral level	3rd exercise ⟷ 4th exercise	
Etheric level	2nd exercise ⟶ 5th exercise	
Physical level	1st exercise ⟷ 6th exercise	

What is important:

- Perceiving and grasping the total exercise organism as a spiritual reality, as spiritually objective.
- Experiencing within yourself the qualities and structure of this exercise.
- Understanding that we are dealing here with a paradox—thinking about thinking itself—but that this is a concrete reality at a higher level of experience.
- Understanding that this exercise enables our normal thinking, feeling and will to be elevated to a higher level.

Levels of attention: When the other five exercises are practised together, then the interrelationships between all of them will become apparent. The individual exercises can then be compared with one another, allowing us to experience the essential quality of each with great assurance and certainty. We can then recognize that the six exercises fall naturally into pairs manifesting on one of the three levels—physical, etheric and astral—and that each pair represents a mutual polarity, one being more related to the person practising it while the other is more related to the world. If we carry out all five exercises in the course of one day, then all six are in fact practised in harmony as one. We can then experience the six-exercise organism, and become aware of its intrinsic nature. (This aspect will be further developed in Chapter 4 in Part Three of this book.)

Practical suggestions: It is almost impossible to carry out this exercise without planning very carefully—preferably in writing—exactly when in the course of the day each exercise will be performed.

Etheric stream: A feeling of deep joy and satisfaction, as though you are expanding beyond your skin, becoming a radiating being raying out from the earth and through the earth into the world of spirit, thus uniting the earth with that world. (This formulation does not derive from Rudolf Steiner.) Love as the power of thinking.

Gesture: The sixth position of 'I think speech'. Radiant human being. Centre and periphery. I.

Effect: This exercise helps us overcome the chaotic, dissolute effect of the Asuras, who most forcefully oppose the human being's development into a spiritual form, into spirit. The strong connection which our strengthened thinking develops to itself also strengthens the spiritual basis of the physical body within itself, at the same time diminishing the effect of gravity on our thinking capacity. The activity of thinking itself is gradually liberated from the immobility of the brain, which allows it to unite with the living and life-giving heart.

The Asuras are more powerful than Ahriman and Lucifer. Ahriman can only affect the etheric body, which is not subject to the strict laws of matter, such as gravity; and Lucifer can only influence the more spiritual astral body, which for example is unaffected by the power of death. The effect of the Asuras, in contrast, reaches right into matter, to the source of matter and form. The Asuras take part in overseeing physical space, in the sense of lords of chaos. They strive to render formless and diffuse everything which possesses form and shape. The positive aspect of their activity is that existence can become non-existence through them, so that something new can arise and the world can evolve further. Yet we must continually oppose and overcome these chaotic forces. This occurs in our bodies where matter is led into a chaotic form and is then built up and formed anew—in the metabolism and the continually regenerating cells. In every moment we are forming our body, although this activity usually remains unconscious. But we can intentionally raise this structuring activity up into our consciousness, by forming thoughts. By forming thoughts, by 'guiding our own thinking' (*Gedankenführung*), we oppose our 'trainers' who are constantly trying to make our thoughts disconnected and haphazard. We are dealing here in fact with the *spatial structuring* of our thoughts, rather than with their logical structuring. In this spatial dimension we can picture thoughts moving in three directions: upwards, on physical, etheric, astral and ego levels; horizontally left and right in polarities; and forwards and backwards in the enhancement and intensification of their power. In contrast to this kind of thinking, logical thinking is always one-dimensional and linear on the physical plane.

In this exercise 'good will' is developed in the thinking, which can overcome the 'bad will' caused by the lords of chaos.

The relationship of the sixth exercise to the first: In this exercise, the thinking strengthened through the first exercise is focused upon itself, uniting with itself and thereby becoming independent and creative. Its active, creative

capacity is directed in the first exercise upon objects—
outwards in other words—and in the sixth exercise upon
itself (inwards) and in the sixth on the other exercises
(outwards).

Spiritual guides: Spirits of Love (Seraphim). They deliver
the physical body from the force of gravity.

Looking at the human being on earth, the physical body
appears as the foundation for earthly life, for incarnation.
Without a body we cannot live on the earth. As the human
being's foundation on earth, the physical body corresponds
to the universal foundation of all existence. This foundation
is pure, universal love. Love is simultaneously the power
and substance of all existence, which streams out from the
Spirits of Love.

From love–substance all parts of the whole, all forms are
shaped as cosmic space, and move in harmonious relationship to one another. The Spirits of Love observe this
space, which is brought into eternal evolution by the Spirits
of Harmony.

'The human being is a thought-being';[5] he is the thought
of the Hierarchies. He has been formed out of thought-
substance. In thinking is revealed the ground of his being.
In the exercise for control of thinking, and in the soul-
harmony exercise, the formation of thoughts becomes the
foundation for the other exercises.

After pointing to the connection of thinking with feeling
(in the fourth exercise), and with the will (in the fifth),
Rudolf Steiner leaves the pupil free in the sixth exercise to
discover the *connection of thinking with itself* — a main theme
of *The Philosophy of Freedom*. For this is the real practice of
love—uniting everything with everything else.

★   ★   ★

8

The Etheric Streams

Each of the six exercises consists of two parts. The first encompasses all that has been described already, while the second involves concentrating upon a delicate, subtle feeling in the astral body at the end of each exercise, corresponding to a particular energy stream of the etheric body—a particular *etheric stream*. Carrying out the exercises in full consciousness is more an astral body activity, while focusing on these subtle sensations is more connected with the etheric body, is more to do with learning to *experience* the etheric streams.

These etheric streams are not the 'normal' ones, which flow through all the chakras—through the acupuncture meridians—and facilitate and direct the physiological life processes of our body. They are, rather, guided and led by the astral body; they work in harmonious confluence with the etheric body's further development, flowing more at the boundary between the etheric and astral body than within the physical body itself. These etheric streams create an anchor-point and basis within the etheric body for the chakras of the astral body. This basis is differentiated in correspondence with the sequence of the chakras, forming a new chakra organism—we can speak in terms of new meridians—by means of which the etheric kundalini can awaken in reverse order, from above downwards. This is why these etheric streams were called 'feelings' by Rudolf Steiner; rightly understood, they are not experienced as physical sensations (which are directly related to the etheric body), since their effect does not extend into the physical body. Their activity at the boundary between etheric and astral body is experienced more as a feeling of energy or force, as a spiritual feeling.

In what follows, the etheric streams will be characterized in Rudolf Steiner's words, and represented pictorially according to my own experience of them.[1]

The first exercise:

At the end of the exercise an endeavour is made to become fully conscious of that inner feeling of firmness and security which will soon be noticed by paying subtler attention to one's own soul; the exercise is then brought to a conclusion by focusing the thinking upon the head and the middle of the spine (brain and spinal cord), as if the feeling of security were being poured into this part of the body.[2]

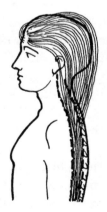

Fig. 11: First etheric stream

This exercise awakens in the pupil a feeling of certainty and steadfastness, since it activates the chakra between the eyebrows. One should send this feeling from that point through the brain and into the spine.[3]

After some time one can then start to notice a feeling of firmness and certainty in the soul. But you must not imagine that this is going to bowl you over. No, it is a very delicate, subtle feeling that you need to listen out carefully for. Those who state that they can find no trace of this feeling within themselves are like someone trying to find a needle in a haystack by trampling about all over it—it is there but they miss it. One must become very still and quiet and listen inwardly, then one can become aware of this feeling, chiefly in the forehead. Once one has sensed it there, one should imagine pouring it into the brain and the spinal column. One can then gradually start to sense streams of energy raying out from the forehead into the spine.[4]

After doing this exercise, one will after a while come to sense a feeling of inner assurance and steadiness. This is a very specific feeling, and one should try to become very aware of it, and then pour it, as though it were water, into the head and spine.[5]

Becoming aware of this feeling should follow directly after the exercise.

The second exercise:

If, through the second exercise, this initiative of action has been achieved, then, with subtle attentiveness, we become conscious of the feeling of an inner impulse of activity in the soul; we pour this feeling into the body,

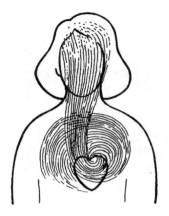

Fig. 12: Second etheric stream

letting it stream down from the head [and over the heart].[6]

Then one can soon notice a feeling arising from doing this exercise, which is something like: 'I'm capable of something', 'I'm more capable than I used to be', and 'I feel an urge to be active'. One actually feels this in the whole upper part of the body. One should then try to allow this feeling to flow down to the heart.[7]

Once more one becomes aware of a certain feeling, a steadiness and an urge to be active. One should raise this feeling into full consciousness, then pour it like water from the head down to the heart, in order to embody it fully.[8]

Once again, the awareness of this feeling should follow immediately after carrying out the exercise.

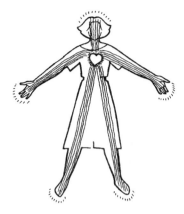

Fig. 13: Third etheric stream

The third exercise:

Above all, if subtle attentiveness is maintained, an inner tranquillity in the body will one day become noticeable; as in the two cases above, we pour this feeling into the body, letting it stream from the heart towards the hands, the feet, and finally the head. This naturally cannot be done after each exercise, for here it is not a matter of one single exercise but of sustained attentiveness to the inner life of the soul. Once every day, at least, this inner tranquillity should be called up before the soul and then the exercise of pouring it out from the heart should proceed.[9]

This gives a feeling of peace, which one allows to stream out from the heart through the arms and hands.[10]

And once one has managed this a few times, one can start to sense a feeling of peace and equanimity. One allows this feeling to flow through the whole body, from the heart through the arms and hands firstly, so that it radiates out from the hands into one's deeds. Then one lets it stream down to the feet, and lastly to the head.[11]

This feeling of peaceful equanimity makes itself felt as an inner warmth. One concentrates it in the heart and allows it to radiate from there out into the hands and feet, and then into the head.[12]

This experience of the etheric stream can conclude your daily quiet time (see Part Two, Chapter 4, 'The Third Exercise').

The fourth exercise:

He who consciously turns his mind, for one month, to the positive aspect of all his experiences will gradually notice a feeling creeping into him as if his skin were becoming porous on all sides, and as if his soul were opening wide to all kinds of secret and delicate processes in his environment which hitherto entirely escaped his notice [...] If it has once been noticed that the feeling

Fig. 14: Fourth etheric stream

described expresses itself in the soul as a kind of bliss, endeavours should be made in thought to guide this feeling to the heart and from there to let it stream into the eyes, and thence out into the space in front of and around oneself. It will be noticed that an intimate relationship to this surrounding space is thereby acquired. A [person] grows out of and beyond himself as it were.[13]

When continued, this exercise gives a feeling of great joy.[14]

Then you can feel as though you are growing beyond your skin. The feeling of expansion and enlargement is similar to the one that the etheric body has after death. When you sense this feeling, let it radiate out through your eyes, ears and the whole surface of your skin.[15]

Then, one day, you will have a feeling of inner bliss. Concentrate it in your heart, let it stream up to your head, and from there out through your eyes, as though you wanted to pour it out through your eyes.[16]

You should let this outstreaming occur each time that you have carried out the exercise, or at least on some occasions.

The fifth exercise:

If he turns his attention, in the fifth month, to developing this attitude of mind, he will notice creeping into his soul a feeling as if something were becoming alive, astir, in the space referred to in connection with the exercise for the fourth month. This feeling is exceedingly delicate and subtle. Efforts must be made to be attentive to this delicate vibration in the environment and to let it stream, as it were, through all the five senses, especially through

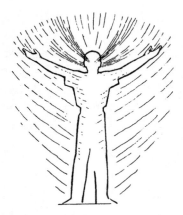

Fig. 15: Fifth etheric stream

the eyes, the ears and through the skin, in so far as the latter contains the sense of warmth.[17]

That gives one a feeling of being able, to some extent, to perceive outside of one's body.[18]

Then a feeling comes over us as though something were streaming into us from outside. We suck it in through eyes, ears and the whole skin.[19]

Then you will soon start to feel as though something is streaming into you from the space outside you. You suck it into yourself, as it were, through eyes, ears and your whole skin.[20]

You should let this feeling arise immediately each time you have carried out the exercise, or at least on some occasions.

The sixth exercise:
(No description written by Steiner is known of.)

By practising this exercise, one will start to feel as though one is growing larger, growing out beyond one's skin.[21]

Fig. 16: Sixth etheric stream

You should allow this feeling to arise immediately after completing the whole exercise.

The etheric stream inner/outer polarity between the first three and the last three exercises is very clear: in the first three the etheric streams remain within the physical body, in the last three they either radiate from within outwards or into us from outside.

★

The etheric streams have been gradually prepared during the course of history. In our time it is becoming necessary to bring them systematically to maturation. The six exercises also contribute to this, as an important contemporary task of spiritual schooling. In the past people had an intuitive awareness of these etheric streams, and at certain times depicted them in symbolic form.

In Roman times the legionaries' helmets were adorned with a kind of brush-tail, a 'bush'. This indicated the power of logical thinking which had reached maturity at that

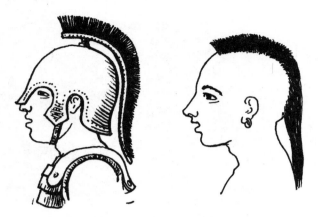

Fig. 17: Symbol of the first etheric stream

time, and which underpinned the strict, logical order and organization of the Roman Empire. Many peoples offered either little or no resistance to the conquering Roman legions; and the reason for this was that a population which still had clairvoyant faculties recognized in this bush a symbol of a new, powerful capacity for logical thinking. The power of thinking must now be raised to a still higher level. In the context of all six exercises, the first exercise serves as a transition from logical thinking to a thinking beyond logic. The Greeks had the same symbol too, as did the Indians and certain European peoples, usually formed from feathers. We can see it today in decadent form in so-called punk hairstyles, where it expresses a striving that has not yet found the right way to fulfil itself.

The breastplates of Roman legionaries were also often adorned over the heart region. In still earlier times the high priests of the Jews wore holy breastplates decorated with precious stones. Later, in the Middle Ages, people—not only priests—wore crosses over the chest and heart region. This symbol also made a deep impression on heathen

Fig. 18: The second etheric stream

peoples, as is shown by the story of Constantine the Great. The modern, widespread habit of wearing pictures and images of all kinds on the front of shirts and blouses is an echo of the subconscious spiritual striving to enliven the heart chakra.

The five-pointed star is also a much used symbol nowadays, appearing on the flags of many countries, on pieces of jewelry, in advertising (see Fig. 19), and in many

Fig. 19: Symbol of the third etheric stream

other situations. As the pentagram it is an image of the whole human being and thus relates to the third etheric stream.

I have not found corresponding symbols for the fourth, fifth and sixth exercises. For the fourth etheric stream one can perhaps think of the image of the sacred heart of Jesus used in Catholic tradition: that of Jesus' visible heart glowing and shining within his breast. Yet this symbolic image, this imagination, is not a widespread, universal one. In recent times, a reality which has increasingly entered the consciousness of many people—for it is valid for all—is the figure of the 'being of light', which everyone encounters at the threshold of death. It is chiefly through the new phenomenon of near-death experience that our encounter with this being has become known—countless people throughout the world have undergone such an experience.[22] This being of light has come to replace the figure of the dark (grim) reaper, the old archetypal image of death. The paradigm of death as the end of life is thus being replaced with the paradigm of death as transformation. Death is no more, it has been overcome! It may well be that in relation to the consciousness developed through the last three exercises, real spirit beings are now coming to take the place of symbols.

*   *   *

9

The Exercise Plan

In this chapter various overall aspects connected with practising the exercises will be discussed.

Preparation and planning

Successful practice of the exercises depends to a large degree on thorough preparation and on making a detailed plan. It is helpful to write down your plan, for which purpose a diary can be useful.

It is a good idea to choose a day for beginning the practice on which you will have enough time for preparation, also one that falls during a period suitable for making a start. Experience has shown that autumn or Michaelmas time is better than summer, spring or winter, especially when beginning the exercises for the first time. This is because autumn is better suited to the concentrated inner work necessary for the first, thinking exercise; and the further sequence of the exercises fit better with the character of the succeeding seasons from that point onwards.

The length of practice does not have to be exactly the same for each exercise. More important is the suitability of the first day—a Sunday for example, or the first day of the month. One should also take holidays and other such periods into account, when it seems that doing the exercises is more difficult.

Before beginning, it is good to develop an overview of

all six exercises, so that you can always retain a perspective of the whole during the course of practice.

You should first ask yourself seriously and soberly whether you really have the will to undertake the exercises and to stick with them to the end. For, from an esoteric perspective, it is better not to start anything than prematurely to break off something you have begun. Most people cannot plumb the supersensible processes at work here; and when such an undertaking is not carried through to the end, a door is opened through which the harmful influences of adversarial powers can gain entry. I do not mean that there is any harm in carrying out an individual exercise wrongly or poorly—in the way Rudolf Steiner gave these exercises that does no damage at all—but that the whole structure and undertaking should be preserved. Carrying out the overall exercise imperfectly and unsatis-factorily is something that helps us learn to live with our own frustrations; and that, in fact, is what enables us to learn at all.

Length of practice

The shortest feasible period for each exercise is two weeks. The necessary length should not be determined in advance; it is best to carry on the exercise until the feeling, the experience of the etheric streams makes itself felt—on average about four weeks. Rudolf Steiner made all sorts of different suggestions: 'for several months', 'for about a month,' 'until the corresponding feeling arises', 'a month or longer', 'at least four weeks', 'even for several months—until one feels that the exercise is bearing fruit', 'these exercises do not have to be carried out for an exact month each. I just had to give some idea of the amount of time', 'one can continue each of these exercises for six to eight weeks, or for as long as seems necessary'.[1]

Anyone who has some experience with these exercises knows that the faculties acquired by doing them for only one exercise period are not yet permanently present. They will be lost rather quickly if one does not keep exercising further. Rudolf Steiner called attention to this in the following words referring to the second exercise although it obviously pertains to the other exercises as well:

> When this [first] exercise has been practised for, say, one month, a second requirement [exercise] should be added ... This exercise, also, should last for one month. But as far as possible during this second month, too, the first exercise should continue, although it is a less paramount duty than in the first month. Nevertheless it must not be left unheeded, for otherwise it will quickly be noticed that the fruits of the first month are lost and the slovenliness of uncontrolled thinking begins again. Care must be taken that once these fruits have been won, they are never again lost.[2]

	1st period	2nd period	3rd period	4th period	5th period	6th period
6th exercise						whole day
5th exercise					whole day	morning
4th exercise				whole day	morning	afternoon
3rd exercise			3–5	3–5	3	3
2nd exercise		3–5 times	3 times	3 times	twice	twice
1st exercise	15–30 min.	10 min.	5 min.	5 min.	5 min.	5 min.

The above plan contains suggestions for carrying out a whole cycle of exercises, including length and regularity of daily practice as well as the best time of day. You should determine the length of each period in accordance with your own life circumstances. When you have completed a cycle, then you should 'start again from the beginning'[3]— either after a pause, or immediately.

Sequence of the exercises

If one takes up the cycle of exercises, they must be done in the exact sequence given. Although this may appear self-evident, in practice people often disregard this basic rule, particularly when, in the enthusiasm of practice, they are tempted to repeat a whole exercise-period which they may consider more important for themselves. Rudolf Steiner expected such temptations to arise:

> The most important thing is to carry out the exercises in this specific sequence. Those who do the second exercise before the first will get nothing out of it. It is the sequence which is important. Some people even think they should begin with the sixth exercise, with the harmonization of all six. But what can you harmonize if there is nothing there yet? Those who fail to carry out the exercises in the right order will get nowhere. It is like taking six steps over a footbridge and trying to take the sixth step first—wanting to begin with the sixth exercise is just as pointless.[4]

A 'trial-run'

A part of the preparation can consist in forming an over-view of what will be required, how the exercises will fit into your day, the efforts needed in relation to other exercises, your own potential and capacities, etc. Before you 'really' begin, you can do a kind of trial-run by going through the exercises, spending, for instance, from two days to a week on each. That will only be useful as a test-run, for such a short time is far from enough to allow each exercise to take effect.

Failing

If you think that you haven't done one or other of the exercises well enough during the allotted period, or if you have failed to do it at all for some length of time, this should *not* prevent you continuing with the exercises in their proper sequence. Just continue as you had planned, and try to carry out that particular exercise better at the next repetition. But to avoid this happening altogether, it can be very helpful to get into the habit of marking it in a pocket diary.

Illness or stressful circumstances, as well as unfamiliar environments, journeys, exhaustion, tiredness, bad moods, etc. can make it very difficult for you to carry out the exercises properly. Instead of giving up altogether at such times, it is good to concentrate at least briefly on the exercise, to hold it in your awareness for a moment. 'Even if you only do this for a minute, it is still of great significance for the rhythm of the physical and etheric body.'[5]

Perfection should not be the aim. Just try to carry out in a serious and sober way what lies within your capacities.

The relationship to other esoteric exercises

What is the relationship of these so-called accompanying exercises to other exercises, for example to the exercises which Rudolf Steiner, in particular contexts, called the 'main exercises'? Let me draw your attention to the following in relation to daily practice.

The six 'accompanying exercises' are, as has been shown already in the first part of this book, the only exercises of this kind which actually have a dual character. On the one hand they are *indispensable* protecting exercises which *must* be practised together with *all* other (main) esoteric exercises—meditation, mantric verses, etc.; on the other hand they are fundamental exercises which directly help the heart chakra to mature, and in consequence contribute decisively to the forming of the new central organ of the human being's bodily sheaths. The task of protection consists in keeping harmful forces from penetrating a person's physical and etheric body, during the time that he is outside these bodies, dwelling only in the astral body and ego, in certain forms of meditation.[6] As fundamental exercises, these six exercises help develop and form the heart chakra—and one cannot emphasize strongly enough that the formation and maturation of this chakra is the most important task of our time. So these exercises have a fully self-contained, intrinsic task, and are therefore independent of any other exercises. As Rudolf Steiner sees it, all the meditations he gave *are actually dependent on the six basic exercises*—not the other way round! The six basic exercises should not be performed in a secondary, lesser way. The term 'accompanying' or 'subsidiary' has of course allowed false conceptions to arise.

★   ★   ★

PART THREE:
THE HEART EXERCISE

1

Overview

In Part Two of this book the six basic exercises were treated as separate, individual exercises. In Part Three I will try to make clear how all six can be viewed as a whole exercise, as a 'heart exercise', and simultaneously carried out as *one* single exercise. First let me draw attention to the special place occupied by these exercises among the other chakra exercises.

In Part One, Chapter 2, on the traditional chakra teaching, I spoke of the creation and development of the eight-petalled chakra. Rudolf Steiner himself, so it seems at first glance, gave no specific exercises for developing this chakra. But in *How to Know Higher Worlds* and *The Stages of Higher Knowledge*, he points to four exercises whose purpose is to establish four 'inner habits' in the soul. These four exercises are intended to enable soul-habits to develop which are indispensable for the creation and development of the new centre within the etheric body. They are variously termed 'faculties', 'attributes' or 'virtues'.

Three of these four exercises are not clearly described—only the third exercise is, consisting of the totality of the six exercises. The six exercises, the heart chakra ones, are therefore referred to in this context as *one single* exercise which allows the third soul faculty to develop. But this soul-habit is intimately connected with the new kind of thinking that is activated by the awakened heart chakra:

Thinking with the heart ... This does not mean [that] the physical heart [thinks] but the spiritual organ that develops in the neighbourhood of the heart, the twelve-petalled lotus-flower [chakra].[1]

The six exercises thus assume their special place in relation to the other chakra exercises—on the one hand as the heart chakra exercises, and on the other as a part of the exercises that form and develop the eight-petalled chakra. (It would go beyond the scope of this book to explain fully that Rudolf Steiner's indications about the development of the other three virtues are in fact the exercises for the two-petalled, sixteen-petalled and ten-petalled chakras, in shortened and concealed form—see Part One, Chapter 3. This means that the four virtues are related to the activity of the upper four chakras; that, in other words, the harmonious interplay of these four chakras wakens the eight-petalled chakra.) In Part Three, Chapter 4, 'The Heart Exercise', I will try to describe a particular way of carrying out this heart exercise.

In the same chapter I will relate the performing of the heart exercise to the fundamental eurythmy exercise which Rudolf Steiner gave to the first eurythmist, Lory Maier-Smits, the so-called 'Agrippa von Nettesheim positions'. They will only be described in as much detail as is necessary for our theme. Therefore this part of the book is aimed mainly at those who have already had actual experience of practising these positions. In Part Three, Chapter 3, 'The Six Gestures', these positions will be explored from a new perspective, again allowing us to see the six exercises as one unity.

★   ★   ★

2

The Six Positions

In 1912, Rudolf Steiner gave six positions as eurythmy exercises, and then in 1924 added accompanying words to them, one phrase for each gesture. These positions were thus broadened from a physical and etheric dimension to a soul-spiritual one, and since then they have been known as 'I think speech ...' (see Fig. 20). In this new form, Steiner recommended them for eurythmy lessons in the following words:

> When one teaches eurythmy to adults and begins by letting them do this particular exercise, they will find their way into the nature of eurythmy far more easily.[1]

He further advised that they be done at every eurythmy performance, just before the performance began and again after it had ended, behind the lowered curtain—not visible to the public, in other words. In both cases—in training and practice, and in connection with the performance of eurythmy, which is itself a kind of meditation, a movement-meditation—this exercise fulfils an essential purpose. It is intended to protect those who do it from the harmful effects that can arise when, just as in meditation, the supersensible sheaths loosen themselves from the body while doing eurythmy. The 'I think speech ...' exercise therefore has the same function in the physical-etheric movement meditation of eurythmy as the 'accompanying' exercises have for soul-spirit meditation. It is a short 'accompanying movement'.

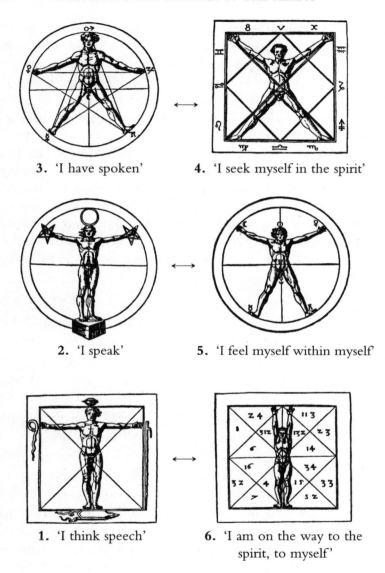

3. 'I have spoken'   **4.** 'I seek myself in the spirit'

2. 'I speak'   **5.** 'I feel myself within myself'

1. 'I think speech'   **6.** 'I am on the way to the
spirit, to myself'

Fig. 20: The Agrippa positions

The organism of the six positions of 'I think speech ...' is structured in the same way as the basic exercises, for instance in the polarity of inner/outer between the first three and the last three positions. The first three are more orientated towards inner bodily space, since the arms remain below the top of the head; the last three are more directed towards external space, the arms being raised above the head. (The French eurythmist Marc Belbéoch also recognized this correlation.[2]) These gestures correspond to the soul-spirit gestures of thinking activity, as well as to the etheric gestures or streams of the accompanying exercises as described in the preceding section of the book.

This similarity becomes still more apparent when we look at the exercises from the perspective of harmonizing the soul capacities, harmonizing thinking, will and feeling in the accompanying exercises and in cases of illness. Rudolf Steiner says:

> This exercise is, when performed as gestures one after another, also one of the curative eurythmy exercises which harmonize the soul. If people are coming apart inwardly in their soul to such a degree that this also comes to physical expression, comes to expression in illnesses of the metabolism, then this exercise is excellent as a curative eurythmy exercise.[3]

Another important similarity between these positions and the accompanying exercises consists in the fact that both are structured according to the seven sheaths of the human being, that is, that they correspond to the sequence leading from the physical body to spirit-man. This has already been demonstrated in relation to the accompanying exercises in Part Two, Chapter 7, 'The Sixth Exercise'. For

the 'I think speech...' exercises, let me quote an experienced eurythmist:

> Looking at the whole sequence, the six positions can be
> seen as 'stations' in which the members of the human
> being create a reflection or image of themselves in space.
> From the midpoint of the exercise in the first position,
> the ego takes hold of the body as physical instrument for
> the word. In the second position it forms the living word
> in the etheric, and in the third grasps inner space for the
> soul, thus giving birth to the instrument for visible
> speech ... In the fourth position, the ideal image of the
> spirit-self is grasped through standing within the spirit. In
> the fifth, the image in space expresses the shining of the
> life-spirit level; and in the sixth position we find an image
> expressing a time when all obstacles will have been
> overcome, an image of the future spirit-man.[4]

It seems possible, in addition, to demonstrate a further
aspect of the resemblance between these positions and the
accompanying exercises, this time more from a soul-spirit
perspective, that is, by looking at the words themselves. I
will elaborate on this in the next chapter, which will help
provide important indications for carrying out the six
accompanying exercises as *one* heart exercise.

★   ★   ★

3

The Six Gestures

The 'gestures' referred to above consist of the content and meaning of the words accompanying the 'I think speech...' positions, broadened and extended in such a way that their relatedness to the six exercises becomes clearer and more easily recognizable. In what follows, therefore, the words and the gestures of the individual positions will be grasped anew in such a way that the inherent *thought-gesture* will be emphasized.

The first gesture:

'I think speech'

a) *The words.* The content of speaking, speech, is the world itself. The spoken word (utterance, sound) or the written word (sign, letters) symbolically represent the perceived objects/beings of our world. Through them the world becomes accessible to the activity of thinking, and can therefore be worked through in symbolic form. These symbol words correspond to our concepts and ideas. All abstract ideas also, such as love, good, the state, etc., are *abstracted* from perception and the experience of

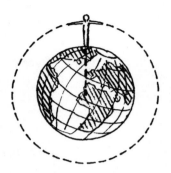

Fig. 21: The first gesture

concrete, material objects: love from the primal experience of the inherent gesture of motherliness; or the state
from interrelationships in the political and social organization of society. Speech or speaking is the vehicle which
carries out into the world these inner concepts living in
the soul. 'I think speech' means: As a unique 'I' I think
about the world from my own unique perspective, which
is simultaneously the place which I, as thinker, occupy on
the earth's surface.

b) The position. The arms, following the surface of the
earth, are spread horizontally, and encompass the earth; the
body orientates itself vertically to the earth's centre. The
gesture of the arms relates to the content of thinking,
speech; and the body to the standpoint or perspective of
thinking—I think—within space. The position appears
here on the physical level.

The second gesture:

'*I speak*'

a) **The words.** The expression 'I speak' points to action *per se*, to the process of will. Through speech, a thought goes out into the world as language, thus appearing as the first manifestation of human will. Only when an idea has been formed as speech can it be transformed into activity. We always think in words and through words, even when these are not audible or visible, that is, written. The thought flows out into the world upon a stream of breath and speech. Speaking unfolds in time, is a time process.

b) **The position.** The arms slightly raised and brought slightly forwards, with the hands at larynx height, point to the organ and activity of speech, a slight leaning forward, and the very slightly spread legs loosen the fixed quality of the first position; action now becomes possible. The power of the etheric body streams forwards.

Fig. 22: The second gesture

The third gesture:

'I have spoken'

*a) **The words.*** After speaking we perceive what we have spoken, and reflect about it. Our feeling life now makes a connection with what has been said. A judgement is spoken by the heart. As a result of our own judgement about what we have said, balance, equanimity rises in the soul.

*b) **The position.*** The hands now sink to heart level, thus ending the first rhythm of shoulder-larynx-heart, and the legs spread wider apart to bring the whole body now leaning slightly backwards to rest in the form of the pentagram. The cross-shape of the first position, after passing through the dynamic transitional moment of the second, is resolved and balanced in the star-form. The star becomes an image of the soul; we have arrived at the astral level.

Fig. 23: The third gesture

The fourth gesture:

'I seek myself in the spirit'

a) The words. In earthly conditions we do not perceive the 'I' in its true form, only as activity of the soul. After the earthly 'I', or self, has been recognized in our experience of thinking, feeling and will—in the first, second and third stances—we now seek the true 'I' in its own world, the world of spirit. We try to do this firstly by recognizing the attributes of the true 'I'—the true, the good and the beautiful—within earthly phenomena.

b) The position. Now spread far apart, the arms and legs are orientated towards infinity, the body as in the third gesture. The straight lines cross in the navel region or radiate out from it, forming parts of a circle which unite in the heavenly sphere of the spirit. Thus is formed the lemniscate between periphery and centre; we seek the self

Fig. 24: The fourth gesture

within it—it creates the path from the earthly to the spiritual 'I' or self.

The fifth gesture:

'I feel myself within myself'

*a) **The words.*** The human being now feels a connection between the spiritual self he has found and his earthly self. His life, hitherto circumscribed by birth and death, now opens to the dimension of spirit. He recognizes the possibility of a reality beyond the boundaries of his previous experience; he tries to act in ways which are in harmony with the future, rather than determined by the past. (The first 'myself' refers to the spirit, the second to the earthly self.)

*b) **The position.*** The connection of the earthly self with

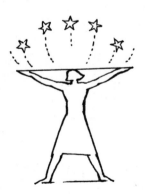

Fig. 25: The fifth gesture

the spiritual self is created through the lemniscate (figure of eight). Hands and legs now come close once more to the body now leaning slightly forward; the hands sink to the level of the top of the head. What is endless thus touches the finite realm, so as to open a path towards the future for the impulses of will.

The sixth gesture:

'I am on the way to the spirit, to myself'

a) The words. Thinking is now no longer directed towards an object, whether material or conceived, but towards the pure interrelationships between such objects. An object exists in space, whereas an interrelationship lives in the

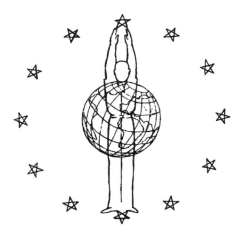

Fig. 26: The sixth gesture

tension *between* objects, in dynamic space, in evolution, in the journey from one to the other. As spirit, the human being is always journeying, evolving, becoming.

(b) The position. The arms are now lifted vertically upwards, the second, reversed rhythm is completed—the arms having passed from the diagonal spread above the head, to the height of the top of the head, to vertically above the head—and the legs are closed once more. The body assumes a vertical, straight, stretched form. The cross of the first position has passed through these various stages to become a ray shining outwards; from the earth it rays out into cosmic space, and from infinity it rays down through the earth. The first position's polarity of periphery/centre has now metamorphosed into the radius of unity. The human ray-being connects the earth and all that is earthly with the spirit, the universe. The human being becomes himself, his own spiritual form.

This last gesture, corresponding with the performance of all six exercises, achieves the maximum intensity. At this point a short summary is in order, to gain an overview of the importance of this last gesture, as well as of the positions, the six exercises and the etheric streams.

In his drawings, in purely esoteric form, Agrippa von Nettesheim drew special attention to the last gesture. On all the drawings one can see other forms besides the human figure (which however have no connection with eurythmy). The drawing for the first position shows concrete objects of symbolic significance: an eye, a stick formed from a branch, a snake and a shield. The second shows a cube, as well as the two geometrical symbols of circle and pentagram. The drawings for the following three positions show symbols for the planets and the zodiac. Only in the sixth and last do numbers appear. These additions not only point to a particular intrinsic content for each position—with close connections to the six exercises—but also to a process of intensification through the sequence: from concrete, earthly objects to geometrical shapes and then, through symbols of the planetary bodies, to symbols for pure interrelationships, for the purely spiritual. (The numbers signify pure form and relationship, not content; number reveals the deepest secrets of Creation.) The drawing for the sixth position thus expresses the conscious elevation of the wise man, of the esotericist, into the realm of pure spirit.

The six etheric streams of the six exercises can also be viewed in the same way. When the last, raylike stream of the sixth position arises, it directs the etheric influence to the vertical central channel of the kundalini. Working with the six etheric streams allows a certain degree of awakening of the kundalini.

A similar effect, but now on the astral level, is achieved by carrying out the six gestures: through them our attention, our consciousness, can step beyond the normal framework of ideas about our physical form. The form and figure of the etheric human being can expand these concepts. The upright form as it appears in the sixth gesture was considered to be the human being's true form in esoteric tradition. This becomes apparent from the following example.

Noah built his ark in measurements with the following ratio: 300 length, to 50 breadth, to 30 height (Moses 6: 13–15). This corresponds to the human body with arms stretched upwards—the breadth of the body being a sixth and its width a tenth of its length. The Egyptians used a corresponding body-measurement, though determined by six circles, as the basis for all other harmonious ratios—including those of the pyramids (see Fig. 27).

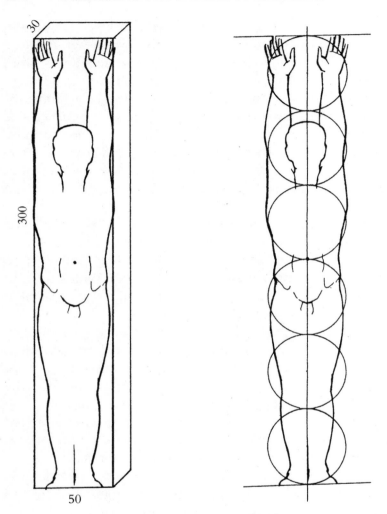

Fig. 27: The Hebraic Ark (left) and the Egyptian circle (right)

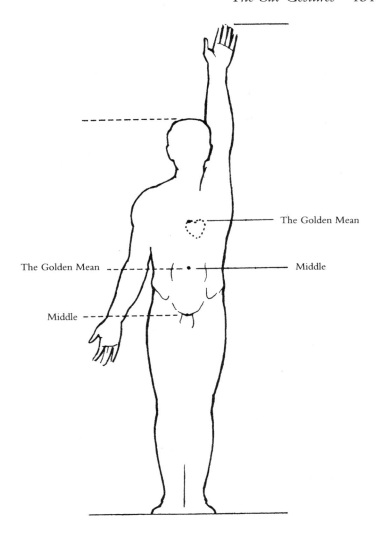

Fig. 28: The Golden Mean in the human form

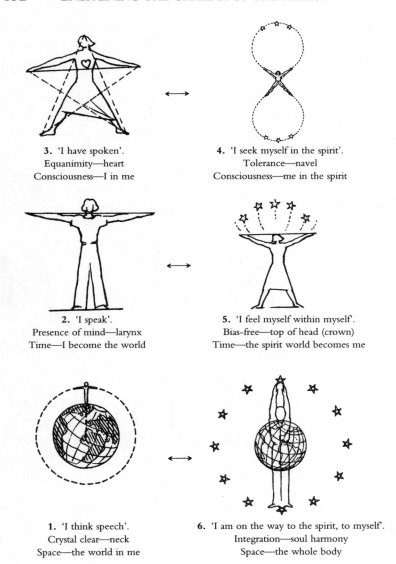

3. 'I have spoken'.
Equanimity—heart
Consciousness—I in me

4. 'I seek myself in the spirit'.
Tolerance—navel
Consciousness—me in the spirit

2. 'I speak'.
Presence of mind—larynx
Time—I become the world

5. 'I feel myself within myself'.
Bias-free—top of head (crown)
Time—the spirit world becomes me

1. 'I think speech'.
Crystal clear—neck
Space—the world in me

6. 'I am on the way to the spirit, to myself'.
Integration—soul harmony
Space—the whole body

Fig. 29: The six gestures

If one compares the 'normal' image of the body as it appears in the first gesture with that of the sixth gesture, two different ratios become apparent.

In the first three gestures the hands and arms always remain below the level of the top of the head. The midpoint of the body, between the top of the head and the soles of the feet, is at the level of the sexual organs: head–sexual organs–earth is a sequence that points to earthly consciousness and thinking. But there is another midpoint, determined in a different way. This discloses a purely spiritual, living interrelationship, and comes about through the 'Golden Mean'. Using this, the navel becomes the midpoint—the point of the body that connects us with pre-birth existence.

In the last three gestures, arms and hands are always above the head. In the sixth gesture, the arithmetical midpoint of the body is located at the navel, between the soles of the feet and the tips of the fingers of the vertically raised arms, and the Golden Mean then lies at the level of the heart—at another 'navel' in other words, the birthplace of the 'I'.

These gestures can be performed just like the eurythmy positions, but by concentrating inwardly on the contents or concepts connected with them. In the following chapter I will look at the heart exercise, in which, through carrying out the six gestures, the six exercises can be integrated into a unified spirit-body exercise.

★   ★   ★

4

The Heart Exercise

In the form described here, the heart exercise does not derive directly from Rudolf Steiner, but was arrived at through my own efforts to get to grips with the six basic exercises. But in the second part of this chapter attention will be drawn to two exercises given by Rudolf Steiner, in which the totality of the six basic exercises appears in a condensed and concentrated form. The following exercise can be seen as a variant of these.

We have seen in the course of this book that the six basic exercises, the Agrippa positions and the six gestures are actually constituent parts of *one* exercise, which can be called the 'heart exercise'. The six basic exercises mainly affect the soul and spirit of the human being, while the positions work more upon the physical and etheric, and the gestures upon the etheric and soul level. Each of these (exercises, positions, gestures) awakens the heart chakra from a different direction and at a different level. They augment and reinforce one another, so that each type of awakening is greatly enhanced. The eurythmy 'I think speech' positions can be carried out in only a few minutes, even if one repeats them several times, as happens on stage before the curtain goes up for a eurythmy performance. The heart exercise can also be successfully performed in a few minutes, but only after long practice, and with the most intense concentration.

This heart exercise is performed by adopting the six gestures one after another in the proper sequence, and simultaneously repeating the six basic exercises inwardly from memory, in an intensive, concentrated and ideal form, by drawing on the soul faculties that have already been acquired through long practice (an advanced exercise).

To do this, it is of course absolutely essential that one has first carried out the cycle of the six basic exercises rigorously and frequently enough—at least seven times—so that one has mastered all their aspects and levels, and in consequence has acquired the necessary soul habits. The same is true also of the gestures.

Practical experience has shown that, after first preparing and testing it for a while, the heart exercise can be carried out in about five minutes. It is best to divide it into three parts and carry it out as follows:

- First of all, carry out the six gestures on their own—for about two to three minutes—by focusing rigorous attention on the physical position, the words and the thought-content of each. Focus as well on the corresponding points of the body: in the first gesture, the point between the shoulder blades; in the second, the larynx; in the third, the heart; in the fourth, the navel; in the fifth, the whole skin surface; and in the sixth gesture, the verticality of the human form itself.
- Secondly, repeat the gestures, again for about two to three minutes, but this time concentrate on the six basic exercises: on thinking, will, feeling; then on thinking within feeling, thinking within will, and lastly thinking within thinking.
- Thirdly, repeat the gestures once more, but focus now

on the etheric streams and the soul moods, and in the following specific way:

1. First etheric stream and an inner feeling of certainty, solidity and truth; you feel rather as though a column or a wall were directly behind your back.
2. Second etheric stream and a feeling of activity, energy and strength; you experience something like a shield, a 'breastplate' in front of your heart.
3. Third etheric stream and a mood of stillness and balance but also of warmth and power, so that you face the world with complete peace and equanimity.
4. Fourth etheric stream and a mood of pouring out love into the world.
5. Fifth etheric stream and a mood of absolute hopefulness, so that you open yourself to the future as it works into the present moment, sacrificing yourself to your own destiny and that of the whole world.
6. Sixth etheric stream and the feeling of unshakeable trust in yourself and the world; a mood of being ready for your own and the world's tasks.

The heart exercise should be carried out from your centre, from the 'I'. One can compare this activity to that of a conductor, who unites all the various different tones and notes of wind instruments and strings in a dynamic harmony. The heart exercise demands activity of a kind which elevates a mere exercise to the level of meditation, in fact to a *dynamic meditation*. This does not just involve a vividly imagined concept, a mantric verse or mantric words, but requires us to bring together gesture, word, concept and etheric stream in a whole meditation organism, and direct our meditative activity to the *interrelation-*

ships between the constituent parts of this organism. The way the exercises are carried out itself becomes a mantric form, is mantrically composed in a way similar to that in which the words of a mantric verse are composed. The heart exercise thus becomes a dynamic meditation, a heart meditation.

It has perhaps become clear by now that these forms of the exercise are carried out on three different levels—the physical, etheric and astral:

- The gestures on the physical level—through focusing upon the body and the natural world.
- The six basic exercises on the etheric level—by recalling the exercises, and actually repeating them in the etheric body; in other words carrying out and thus renewing the same exercise processes once more.
- The etheric streams on the astral level—these are now grasped in a conscious way, and experienced as delicate feelings or soul moods.

The perspective described here is a dynamic one inasmuch as it directs our attention to the integration of the separate constituent elements of the heart exercise or heart meditation. But there is also a second, more static, content-oriented perspective which should be clearly distinguished from the first, and which allows us to perceive the true nature of the heart exercise itself. In this, the gestures or positions lie on the physical level, the etheric streams naturally on the etheric level, and the six exercises, which relate to the soul faculties of thinking, will and feeling, on the soul or astral level. The heart meditation organism is summarized in the schematic form reproduced here (see Fig. 30).

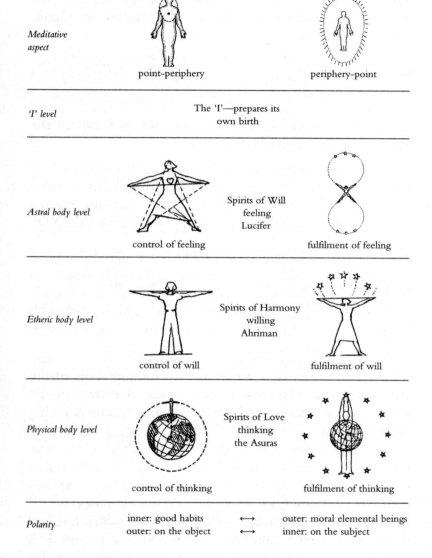

Meditative aspect	point-periphery	periphery-point
'I' level	The 'I'—prepares its own birth	
Astral body level	control of feeling	Spirits of Will feeling Lucifer	fulfilment of feeling
Etheric body level	control of will	Spirits of Harmony willing Ahriman	fulfilment of will
Physical body level	control of thinking	Spirits of Love thinking the Asuras	fulfilment of thinking
Polarity	inner: good habits ⟷ outer: on the object ⟷		outer: moral elemental beings inner: on the subject

Fig. 30: A schematic summary of the heart exercise

The strengthened soul faculties (thinking, will, feeling) outweigh the adversary powers: the Asuras, Ahriman, Lucifer.

The beings of the highest Hierarchies (Seraphim, Cherubim, Thrones) help to transform the physical, etheric and astral body in the spirit-man, life-spirit and spirit-self.

The gestures manifest the outer movement forms of the inner thought forms of the exercises.

The 'control' of thinking, will and feeling becomes 'fulfilment' when our ordinary, everyday consciousness elevates itself to intensive thinking, so that our normal feeling, will and thinking are imbued with pure thinking.

The essence of the six exercises lies in 'I'-activity which, deriving from the level of pure spirit ('I'-level), first turns inwards (point), but whose object of awareness lies outside itself, and then directs itself outwards (periphery)—though it must still, simultaneously, remain aware of inner activity. (See also the following section.)

Through focusing on outer 'objects', good habits of soul are created within, while in the outer realm elemental beings arise who are imbued with my moral forces. This is an 'I'-exercise.

★

At this point I will draw attention to two exercises given by Rudolf Steiner that relate to the heart exercise described above, or of which these may be regarded as a variant. The first is 'Steadfastly I take my place on earth. . .' the second is the meditation 'In me is God—I am in God', from the

Curative Education Course,[1] also known as the 'point/periphery meditation'.

The exercise 'Steadfastly I take my place on earth...' appears as the 13th in the section of 'Main Exercises' in the German edition of *Guidance in Esoteric Training.*[2] This exercise, given to a particular pupil, consists of a mantric phrase and body position (absent from the English edition), to be carried out simultaneously in the morning, and to be recalled in the evening as part of the review exercise of the events of the day. It takes the following form:

Steadfastness	left leg
Certainty	right leg
Strength	heart
Love	left arm
Hope	right arm
Trust	head

Steadfastly I take my place on earth:	concentrate on left leg
Certain as I walk through life:	concentrate on right leg
Strength pours into my heart:	concentrate on the heart
Love I hold in the core of my being:	concentrate on left arm
Hope I imbue in all I do:	concentrate on right arm
Trust I put in all my thinking:	concentrate on head

These *six* go with me through life.

This main exercise is divided into two parts. The first three lines draw our attention to the lower part of the body (legs) and to the heart, while the last three focus on the upper part (arms and head). This gives rise to the following polarities:

3. Strength flows into my heart $\longleftrightarrow$ **4.** I hold love in the core of my being

2. I walk with certainty through life $\longleftrightarrow$ **5.** I imbue all I do with hope

1. Steadfastly I take my place on earth $\longleftrightarrow$ **6.** I put trust in all my thinking

This structure reveals a correspondence with the six accompanying exercises:

taking one's place steadfastly on earth—'down to earth' thinking, appropriate for earthly existence;
walking with certainty through life—initiative in one's actions;
strength flowing into the heart—equanimity, balance, soul harmony;
love in the core of one's being—seeing all that is positive in the world;
imbuing all action with hope—allowing the future to enter one's deeds;
putting trust in all thinking—thinking perceives itself.

These six therefore accompany the pupil to whom they are given through life and protect him, in a similar way to the basic exercises. In both cases the pupil experiences a metamorphosis of an outer stance—steadfastness, certainty, strength—into the inner, Christian virtues of love, hope and faith (trust).

The second exercise was given as a fundamental meditation

for those, such as teachers, who educate other human beings.

In general people fail to achieve anything in the realm of pedagogy because they never manage to awaken a certain truth in themselves, or treat it seriously enough. To do justice to this truth they would need to immerse themselves in the evening in this consciousness: In me is God; God, or the spirit of God, or whatever you like to call it, is in me. But not just chatter theoretically—for most people's meditations are simply theoretical chatter and bibble-babble. And in the morning, so that it streams out and invigorates the whole coming day, one should think: I am in God. Just think for a moment what you are really doing when you waken these two concepts, which also become fully imbued with feeling, yes, also become impulses of will. What you are doing is to place before you this image: In me is God; and then the following morning to have before you the image: I am in God— both are one and the same, both drawings [see Fig. 31]. And what you must understand is that in both cases we have a circle and a point, but that this does not emerge in the evening, only in the morning. In the morning you

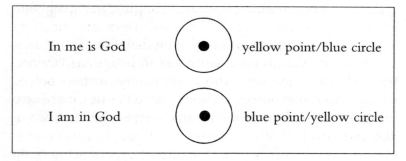

Fig. 31

must think: there is a circle, there is a point. You must understand that a circle can be a point and a point a circle—you must understand this deeply, inwardly.[3]

This exercise can be carried out as a vivid image in one of two ways: as a geometric transformation of the point into the periphery, and vice versa; and as a metamorphosis of yellow into blue and vice versa. The following suggestions (there are, I'm sure, other ways of doing it) may be helpful to the reader.

For the geometrical transformation you can imagine a white point and a white circle on a black background. When you try to 'stretch' the point and at the same time to shrink the circle, both forms will for a moment become one and the same somewhere in the 'middle'—which is, however, less than half of the original distance between them. The outer boundary of the 'point' will become identical with the circle, and as the process continues the circle will contract into a point while the point expands into a 'circle'.

The colour transformation occurs in the same way—you imagine the enlarging yellow point and the contracting blue circle until they become one. At this moment a green circle will appear, as a synthesis of both the original point and circle. Then a yellow circle will continue to expand out of this green circle, while a blue point contracts out of it. The same can be done in the reverse direction.

This is simultaneously a word *and* an image meditation, both of which are once more subdivided in two halves (parts) within themselves. It should therefore be carried out on two levels—both concept and image—but in such a way that one half of it is always transformed or metamorphosed into the other, with the aim of experiencing both halves as one and the same.

The first half represents waking consciousness in the words 'In me is God', in my sense of the 'I' within, and in the picture of the 'I'-point (yellow) in the middle of my body (blue circle). This experience must then be taken into sleep. The second half shows the nature of sleeping consciousness: 'I am in God'. During sleep, in other words, my 'I'-point (blue) is embedded in the world of spirit, in the spirit of God (yellow circle). And that, in turn, must be carried over into waking consciousness. These two parts of the meditation correspond to both perspectives of the human bodily sheaths—inwards and outwards—as was described in Part One, Chapter 1 on 'Method'.[4]

This meditation therefore consists in *inverting or transforming* one half into the other, in the morning in one direction, and in the evening in the other—if one wants to do it properly, rather than just in a 'theoretical bibble-babble' way. This word and image meditation thereby rises to a *dynamic* level of meditation, at which all that is brought together in the 'heart exercise' and in the 'Steadfast...' exercise becomes focused in a process of metamorphosis. The last two exercises are in this sense *dynamic meditations*.

★   ★   ★

PART FOUR:
THE NEW HEART-THINKING

The logic of thinking is compatible with the strongest egotism. The logic of the heart is capable of gradually overcoming all egotism, and uniting all people as participants in a single human community.

Rudolf Steiner

1

Rudolf Steiner's Heart-Thinking

As both earthly and spiritual beings, we are thought-beings; our consciousness is a thinking consciousness operating on two levels—those of sleeping and waking.

During the evolution of humanity, in its descent from the worlds of spirit into earthly existence, and back again to complete reintegration with the spiritual world, the human being, as an incarnating being, evolves only two kinds of thinking.

The essential character of both these kinds of thinking, as well as the nature of the physical organs supporting them, can be described as follows. The first is a purely logical, linear, dead, shadowy thinking dependent upon sense-perceptions, one that until now has been regarded as normal and ordinary, while the second is one that goes beyond logic, is rhythmic or wavelike—a living and independent thinking that is new and that will gradually evolve to be the normal and most widespread kind. In comparison with the second, the first appears as a passive and observing form of consciousness, while the second will manifest as active, living, creative thinking.

These two types of thought-faculty are radically different from one another, and various degrees of perfection can be distinguished within each. The levels of perfection in development of the new thinking have been described by Rudolf Steiner as Imagination, Inspiration and Intuition.

'Thinking' usually refers only to logical thought, which is the third and highest level of the 'old' way of thinking. There are no commonly recognized terms for the other two levels (and to describe them would go beyond the scope of this chapter).

Of the many aspects in which the two kinds of thinking can be observed, I will cite only the following.

In the Bible the two forms of thinking appear symbolized as the two Trees of Paradise: as the Tree of the Knowledge of Good and Evil—which, as a result of man eating its fruit, allowed him to enter earthly existence and become mortal (Genesis 1, Moses 2 and 3); and as the Tree of Life, whose fruit will enable the human being to overcome death and be raised into the New Jerusalem, the new Paradise (Revelation of St John, 1 and 22).

In Rudolf Steiner's science of the spirit, four universal etheric forces are spoken of, four kinds of ether. The two lower kinds—warmth and light ether—are the generating power that makes possible the processes of logical thinking (brain thinking), while the two higher—sound and life ether—make possible the processes of 'supra-logical'[1] thinking—'heart-thinking'.

Seen from the perspective of anatomy and physiology, the brain and nervous system serve logical thinking, while the rhythmic system (heart and lungs) serve supra-logical thinking.

In the brain and nervous system the neurones are the material, physical building blocks for the structure of the thinking process. The corresponding 'building blocks' of the rhythmic system are waves and vibrations, the rhythms of pulse and breathing—not physical entities, therefore, but the *pure forms* of the processes (apart from the material particles carried by these waves).

The new, supra-logical thinking is a purely spiritual thinking. It was first brought to the earth from the world of spirit by Christ, and implanted into the earth by the Deed of Golgotha. It is the Logos-thinking, through which our normal, logical thinking will be resurrected; it is Christian thinking *per se*.

This thinking appeared for the first time in a wholly consistent and independent form, as pure and conscious activity of the etheric body, in Rudolf Steiner. The organ supporting this activity was not the brain but the heart, in other words the physiology of breathing and circulation. This kind of thinking can therefore be called etheric body thinking or heart-thinking:

> In the year 1893, it became necessary for me to write the book *The Philosophy of Spiritual Activity*. It is not the contents of this book that are so important, though obviously at that time one wished to tell the world what is said in it, but the most important thing is that independent thinking appeared in this book for the first time. No one can possibly understand this book who does not think independently. From the beginning, page by page, a reader must become accustomed to using his etheric body if he would think the thoughts in this book at all. Hence this book is a means of education—a very important means—and must be taken up as such.[2]

This thinking was described by Rudolf Steiner in various different ways, each of which characterizes a particular aspect—of Imagination, Inspiration or Intuition. For example: organic-living, living, artistic, intuitive, musical, morphological, thinking with the heart or the breast, thinking with the etheric body, letting the Michaelic quality flow into one's heart.

Rudolf Steiner used this kind of thinking in a wholly conscious and consistent way, radiating his living thoughts directly from the heart, from the etheric body outwards. But most of those who received the thoughts he mediated in this way could only find in them a kind of feeling, a spiritual or heart warmth, rather than recognizing them as thoughts or conceptual content. To make them recognizable, therefore, Rudolf Steiner had to turn this heart-thinking into 'brain thinking', into logical thinking in other words, translating heart language into normal German:

> When [the spiritual researcher into the spirit world] wants to communicate to other human beings what he has experienced through the thinking of the heart, he must translate it into logical thoughts.[3]

Two kinds of thinking and two 'languages' were therefore used by Rudolf Steiner: on the physical level, logical thinking and the German language; on the etheric level, a universally human heart-thinking and the common language of the human heart. The latter can nowadays be perceived and recognized behind the words or content of his writings and lectures, as a higher, though still veiled level.

The fact that heart-thinking is completely different in nature from brain thinking is the reason why most people cannot perceive it—for it is very difficult indeed for normal thought-consciousness to understand. Really to grasp it, one must first develop the requisite physical organs and corresponding thinking capacities. In most people these preconditions have not yet evolved. This is also clear from the following reports, which bear witness to Rudolf Steiner's heart-thinking capacity:

> My husband asked the master (Rudolf Steiner) why it

was that most listeners became sleepy during his lectures. He replied that this was due to the difficult and unfamiliar trains of thought.[4]

What I mention here is not mere fantasy, but a fact that can be corroborated by the experience of dozens, hundreds even, of listeners at various lectures. 'It' did not begin straight away at the first lecture, but only after several; and 'it' was eventually overcome once one developed the capacity to hear with two pairs of ears as it were, to understand in two different ways at the same time. 'It' was the following: as a relatively new, naive listener, and precisely at the very moment of deepest soul upheaval, one was overpowered by an irresistible urge to fall asleep. Such naive listeners fell asleep in large numbers—not through lack of attentiveness, but from an intensification and excess of it, which exhausted the as yet imperfectly developed powers of attention. In lectures which the Doctor (Rudolf Steiner) gave for members only, only a power of attention schooled through the practice of meditation could last out. Without such preparation one would simply be overpowered by sleep, a fact proved by hundreds of instances of it. This even gave rise to the tradition of afterwards comforting those who had fallen asleep and were ashamed of themselves as a result. People would be consoled in such words as: 'Don't worry, that is no ordinary sleep; and the Doctor will certainly not mind, nor anyone else—we've all had the same experience.' I too have been comforted in this way, and comforted others in turn. The phenomenon was explained by a shift in the rhythms of the etheric body, which only gradually accustomed itself to the strong 'dose of Steiner'.[5]

⋆   ⋆   ⋆

2

Rudolf Steiner's Two Paths of Esotericism

The six basic exercises which together compose the heart exercise were first described by Rudolf Steiner in *How to Know Higher Worlds* (1904), then in *The Stages of Higher Knowledge* (1905), and finally in *Occult Science—an Outline* (1909). After describing them for the third time in the fifth chapter of *Occult Science*, 'Knowledge of Higher Worlds', he pointed in the same chapter to two paths of schooling that would allow safe entry to higher worlds—through attaining a 'sense-free thinking', and the 'inner trustworthiness of imaginative knowledge'. The following passage is the last paragraph in the third section of that chapter (pp. 255–256). Rudolf Steiner places this whole paragraph in brackets, but one should by no means think that what is contained there is less important—the opposite is actually the case. Rudolf Steiner often placed his most important statements in slightly concealed places—in forewords or afterwords, or in brackets.

(The path that leads to sense-free thinking by way of the communications of spiritual science is thoroughly reliable and sure. There is however another that is even more sure, and above all more exact; at the same time, it is for many people also more difficult. The path in question is set forth in my books *The Theory of Knowledge Implicit in Goethe's World-Conception* and *The Philosophy of Spiritual Activity*. These books tell of what man's thinking can achieve when directed not to impressions that come from the outer world of the physical senses but *solely upon itself.* When this is so, we have within us no longer the kind of thinking that concerns itself merely with memories of the things of the sense; we have instead *pure thinking* which is like a being that has life within itself. In the above-mentioned books you will find nothing at all that is derived from communications of spiritual science. They testify to the fact that pure thinking, working within itself alone, can throw light on the great questions of life—questions concerning the universe and man. The books thus occupy a significant intermediate position between knowledge of the sense-world and knowledge of the spiritual world. What they offer is what thinking can attain when it rises above sense-observation, yet still holds back from entering upon spiritual, supersensible research. One who wholeheartedly pursues the train of thought indicated in these books is already in the spiritual world; only it makes itself known to him as a thought-world. Whoever feels ready to enter upon this intermediate path of development will be taking a safe and sure road, and it will leave with him a feeling in regard to the higher world that will bear rich fruit in all time to come.)

The *first path* mentioned here—a path for which the practice of the basic exercises is absolutely necessary preparation—is *not* regarded by Rudolf Steiner himself as the more profound one. The more profound and the truly modern one is the *second path*: it is the 'more sure' because it avoids the danger of subjective mental representations, concepts and ideas; it is 'more exact' because it is built on an objective, pure thinking, the heart-thinking; it is 'more difficult' because it requires a kind of 'dying' of logical thinking, a getting out of one's head. Rudolf Steiner describes this new path, which he first opened, in his *Philosophy of Freedom* ('*Freehood*').[1] It is the path upon which the faculty of heart thinking can best be developed. The chakras can develop on both paths, but on the second they do not need to be directly referred to.

How should we understand this evaluation by Rudolf Steiner of these two paths? Four decisive differences between them can provide the basis for such understanding.

I

The surest and most immediate path for the spiritual pupil to attain such sense-free thinking can be the one upon which he makes the realities of the higher world, communicated to him through spiritual science, into the property of his own thinking. These realities cannot be observed by means of the physical senses. Yet one will notice that one can *understand* them, as long as one applies sufficient patience and persistence. Without higher schooling one cannot explore the higher world, cannot make one's own observations about it; but one can understand everything that spiritual researchers reveal about it, without having first undergone such schooling.[2]

To *understand* these communications, however, the esoteric pupil has to gain knowledge of them by working through the concepts already at his disposal and subjecting them to logical thought. The esoteric pupil who cannot arrive at knowledge of higher worlds through his own direct observations will therefore be dependent both on the spiritual researcher and on his own sense-perceptions, by means of which he can understand the communications of the former. On the first path, therefore, attaining the sought-for understanding will always require us to rely on the crutches of sense-derived concepts and mental representations, without which logical thinking cannot function.

In contrast to the first, the second, less immediately accessible path is characterized by its complete, intrinsic freedom from sense-perceptions. Since the heart rather than the brain is used on this path as instrument of the thinking processes, logical thought is replaced by sense-free heart-thinking, uninfluenced by the senses and free of mental representations. This is also why this path is more difficult than the other; it is wholly new, and when one sets out upon it one does not yet have the necessary kind of thinking at one's disposal. As one begins this journey, one has at the same time to create one's own means for progressing along it. On the second path (that of *The Philosophy of Freedom*), one gradually develops heart-thinking—not through understanding the content of the book, but through struggling with its 'dry, mathematical style', in 'inner upheaval, tensions and resolutions'.[3] The aim of the first path, of mental representations, concept and idea, is eventually to lead into the second, sense-free path: the first path leads from the realm of sense-experience *into* the realm of spirit-experience, while the second path takes its starting-point already *from* that higher realm of spirit-experience.

II

From the perspective of human evolution, the first path (of spiritual schooling) is suited to our descent into material, earthly existence. This kind of training must always lead into the realm of 'mystical death'. The second path on the other hand is there to lead us up into the world of spirit, into pure existence. On this path we *have to* pass through the death of the old way of thinking, thus overcoming it and experiencing our resurrection in the new thinking.

Today and for a good while still, both paths will continue to run alongside each other, but only the second path is really suited to our times.

Since there are people who wish, for reasons important to them (destiny), to travel upon the first path, it was necessary to *reform this anew* for our time. This is what Rudolf Steiner achieved at the beginning of this century. In the writings already copiously referred to in this book, he renewed the old esoteric path to facilitate the chakras' continued evolution. This *renewed path* is more certain than the traditional one, which is now not without attendant dangers and does not have future potential—as one can so often see from the 'casualties' of the New Age movement. In contrast to this ancient path of schooling, Rudolf Steiner opened up the *really new path*.

This new path is the Michaelic one, connected with the Tree of Life. It was initiated through the Micha-El event, to make passable for the *real* new age the direct but steep and arduous path to higher worlds. At the time this path was opened, Rudolf Steiner founded a *new esotericism* and a new esoteric schooling. (This new esotericism of the *Philosophy of Freedom* [*'Freehood'*] appeared at the time that the old esotericism became public—that is, exoteric—especially through the writings of H.P. Blavatsky and Rudolf Steiner at the end of the last century.)

III

Since the end of the last century, then, a choice has been available between two esoteric paths of schooling, two kinds of esotericism. The life of the painter August Ewerbeck (1885–1961) provides one illustration of this. He was a friend of Rudolf Steiner and since 1904 had been a member of the Theosophical Society. The following passage comes from a short obituary by Karl Köller:

> From Rudolf Steiner he also received written tasks: he was advised, for example, to work out 'the relationship between thinking and being'. [...] In the first decade of our century, Ewerbeck got word that there were intimate circles in which Rudolf Steiner gave special esoteric training to those admitted to them. So he asked his teacher whether he too might be allowed to attend, and received the astonishing reply: 'You don't need to! You have understood my *Philosophy of Freedom!*'

IV

From an historical point of view, the 'second' or *new esoteric* path of schooling was founded through the publication in 1893 of Steiner's *Philosophy of Freedom*—in other words *before* the 'first' or traditional path was renewed for the world at large by *How to Know Higher Worlds*, published in 1904. The second path of schooling is founded upon the heart-thinking of *The Philosophy of Freedom*. Yet this was not recognized by most of his pupils at that time—and this underlying aspect of it remained an esoteric and secret one. Besides giving a large number of more or less direct hints and indications, Rudolf Steiner continually and expressly tried to draw *The Philosophy of Freedom* to the attention of those esoteric pupils (particularly the members of the Theosophical and later the Anthroposophical Society) who had entered only upon the renewed esoteric path:

People have not managed to read *The Philosophy of Freedom* in a different way from other books. And that is what is needed, and must be emphasized in no uncertain terms, for otherwise the development of the Anthroposophical Society will lag far behind the development of anthroposophy. In which case anthroposophy, taking a round-about path through the Anthroposophical Society, will be wholly misunderstood by the world—and nothing can result from this but conflict upon conflict![4]

But such pointers seem to have been continually overlooked. Towards the end of his life Rudolf Steiner indicated many times that heart-thinking, the true esoteric aspect of *The Philosophy of Freedom*, still remained undiscovered: 'This is the reason why, in *The Philosophy of Freedom*—though most people completely fail to notice it—there is a mood which continually touches into the artistic [thinking] element.'[5]

★

This all goes to show not only that heart-thinking is of the greatest importance, and a radically new phenomenon, but also that this 'primal source' from which all future developments will evolve was opened up *before* the old path was renewed. From heart-thinking Rudolf Steiner first formed the truly esoteric schooling path of *The Philosophy of Freedom*, the 'second' path; and only afterwards did he renew the ancient, 'first' path, which has become known as the 'anthroposophical path of schooling'. The secret of this timing connected with the appearance of heart-thinking is that heart-thinking was the purpose and consequence of Rudolf Steiner's Micha-El initiation which took place during the Holy Nights of 1879/80.

★   ★   ★

3

Special Aspects of Spiritual Schooling

I

I have so far tried to shed light on the nature and task of the so-called basic exercises, the kind of thinking appropriate to them, and their importance for the anthroposophical path of schooling—all from the perspective of a student of Rudolf Steiner's anthroposophy. From the first moment that one sets out upon this path of *schooling*, the question about a teacher and one's relationship to him/her must be answered if the learning process is to develop in a healthy and fruitful way. Like all other schooling, an esoteric one requires a teacher-student relationship—this is no different in self-education, except that then the teacher and the taught are one and the same person.

The question about the need for a teacher—in this case, in connection with the basic exercises—was answered by Rudolf Steiner in a general and affirmative way. That these exercises should be carried out only in the context of a teacher-student relationship was stated in the two basic texts on this theme: at the very beginning of the chapter 'Some Effects of Initiation' in *How to Know Higher Worlds*; and in the first chapter of *The Stages of Higher Knowledge*, in which the exercises for developing the chakras are described. This condition is formulated as follows:

> One of the basic principles of true esoteric science is that those who dedicate themselves to it must do so in full

consciousness. As students, we should undertake nothing, nor engage in any exercises, the effects of which we
do not understand. An esoteric teacher ['Guru' was the
term used by Rudolf Steiner in the early editions], when
giving advice or instruction, will always explain what the
effects of following the instruction will be on the body,
soul or spirit of the person striving for higher knowledge.[1]

In these essays about higher knowledge it has often been
mentioned that specific indications about such exercises
are only passed from one individual to another. No one
should undertake these exercises without guidance, for
only someone who has the right experience in this realm
can assess what effect will be produced on a particular
individual when he undertakes to withdraw the work of
his soul from his body, and to apply it in a higher kind of
activity.[2]

The requirement expressed here by Rudolf Steiner
does not apply in all circumstances. It relates only to the
chakra exercises described in the chapter 'Some Effects of
Initiation' in *How to Know Higher Worlds*, and not to the
exercises described in the preceding chapters. These latter
are entirely commensurate with normal logical thinking,
and therefore require neither super-logical thinking nor a
clairvoyant teacher. But for the chakra exercises this condition remains valid; it was not altered in the later edi-
tions of *How to Know Higher Worlds*. The view that
Rudolf Steiner changed his mind and reversed this stipu-
lation in the 'Afterword' to the 1918 edition seems to me
unfounded. At the end of this chapter I will try to substantiate this opinion.

II

The condition that one should not enter upon a path of schooling without a teacher's guidance implies a very personal, direct form of communication between spiritual teacher and pupil. Not general instruction but a thoroughly individual kind of guidance is necessary for enlivening spiritual organs (chakras), adapted to the specific configuration of each particular person. A teacher, therefore, should always provide advice or instruction only through personal communication between him/herself and the pupil, either in conversation or in a written form—the latter, though, should always be expressed in personal terms, such as a personal letter.

All of this goes to show that such communications are not suited to general publication. The instructions that Rudolf Steiner gave to his pupils cannot be transferred to other pupils or thought of as general *instructions*, even if they are published. What answers the needs and developmental goals of one individual is by no means necessarily suited to those of a small group of people or another individual, for *every single person is unique*. Such a perspective will call into question the way in which the published 'esoteric legacy' of Rudolf Steiner was understood by those seeking an esoteric schooling.

The fact that *How to Know Higher Worlds, The Stages of Higher Knowledge*, and *Occult Science—an Outline* were written with the general public in mind means that they should only communicate a general kind of knowledge, and were not intended as instruction to aid the self-development of specific people. Rudolf Steiner himself described these books as 'theosophical handbooks',[3] and not as theosophical, anthroposophical or esoteric training texts. (A handbook always relates to a subject and not to the user. Instructions can only relate to a certain pupil when they are specifically adapted for him or her from the general facts described in the handbook.) In contrast to these texts, there is another book by Rudolf Steiner which tells of his personal experience on such a path: [*The Philosophy of Freedom*] 'is not intended to be "the only possible" path to the truth; rather it sets out to *describe* the path upon which one person who is concerned with truth has travelled.'[4] This book can really be regarded as an open letter to the world; it communicates concrete exercises and experiences which are suitable for other spiritual students to follow.

One must distinguish quite clearly between the communication of facts or general instructions suitable for many or all people, and of instructions and guidance for the self-development of a particular individual relevant to him or her alone. In the first case, general scientific principles are mainly drawn on, while in the second an artistic forming and creation is at work. The following passage shows how Rudolf Steiner himself describes this distinction, so necessary for an esoteric schooling:

> In a book such as *How to Know Higher Worlds*, one can really only communicate what is to be said about human development in a way that is applicable to each and every human individual who sets out on a path towards the higher worlds. In consequence, such a book inevitably acquires a more abstract, semi-theoretical character, however many specific instances it describes. For of one thing we must be clear: self-development is not the same in each case! There is no self-development as such, no general self-development, but only of this or that or the other person, and of every single, different individual.

There must be as many different processes of self-development in the world as there are human beings. This is why the truest description of a general path of occult knowledge must be characterized by the way it is *not* identical with any single, individual path of self-development. If one wants to describe self-development truly as it appears to perception of the world of spirit, this can only happen by describing the self-development of a single individual, by transposing into individual terms what is universally true for all. Whereas *How to Know Higher Worlds* contains the starting-point of the secret of every human being's self-development, in the Rosicrucian Mystery Play is contained the secret of that of one single individual, Johannes Thomasius. So all that is contained in the laws of occult development had to travel a long way before it could be expressed in terms of a single, real human being. And in the process, on this path, something that is contained in this 'knowledge of higher worlds', and that can become theoretical, had to be almost wholly turned around, reversed.[5]

In the book *How to Know Higher Worlds* is described the path of self-development as it can be seen in every human being—in the only way, therefore, in which this general path can be portrayed. When one describes Johannes Thomasius, on the other hand, a single human being is represented. But in so doing one must deny oneself the possibility of describing self-development in general.[6]

(These extracts are from lectures that Rudolf Steiner gave in connection with performances of his first Mystery Play, *The Portal of Initiation*.)

Friedrich Rittelmeyer, the well-known anthroposophist and intimate spiritual pupil of Rudolf Steiner, drew attention to the particular reasons why only very individual forms of exercises or exercise-systems are suited to each specific person:

> If Rudolf Steiner considered that individual people, by reason of their gifts and their fate, were fitted to be brought into closer connection with the revelations of the spiritual world, he gave them spiritual exercises which formed a complete system suited to these individual people . . .
>
> For the direct development of the spiritual organs of perception described in his book *Knowledge of the Higher Worlds and its Attainment [How to Know Higher Worlds]*, Rudolf Steiner very seldom gave advice, and then only to very few people, under strict preliminary moral conditions.[7]

III

In the 'Afterword' to *How to Know Higher Worlds*, the following nine-sentence paragraph is to be found, which seems to me of decisive importance for satisfactorily answering the question about a personal teacher:

> Readers should approach this book as though they were having a conversation with the author. Therefore the advice about receiving personal instruction on the path to higher knowledge should be understood to refer to this book. In the past, there were good reasons for restricting personal instruction to oral teaching; now, however, we have reached a stage of human development when spiritual-scientific teachings and knowledge

must be spread abroad much more widely than ever before. Its teachings must become much more widely accessible than they were in the past. For this reason the book must take the place of oral instruction. The belief that we need personal instruction in addition to what is said in this book is true only to a limited extent. Some of us may indeed need some additional personal help, and such further instruction may be helpful and meaningful to the individuals concerned. But it would be wrong to think that anything of importance has been left out of this book. Everything may be found in this book if only we read it properly, and above all, *completely.*[8]

As a result of this passage, the view has arisen that Rudolf Steiner wished to say that the spiritual teacher could be replaced by a book. It is quite understandable that such a view has arisen among many readers, for this is what Steiner *seems* to be saying in the central sentence of the paragraph: '*For this reason the book must take the place of oral instruction.*' And yet he has, nonetheless, *not* revoked the introductory sentence of the chapter 'Some Effects of Initiation', in which the need for a personal teacher is affirmed. How are we to understand this apparent contradiction? The composition of the above paragraph holds the first key to answering this question. The first and the last, ninth, sentences of the paragraph stand in a symmetrical relationship to the central, fifth, sentence: '*Readers should approach this book as though they were having a conversation with the author*' and '*Everything may be found in this book if only we read it properly, and above all,* completely.' A closer examination of these sentences—which are often overlooked—can show us the following.

The advice to read the book in a 'proper and complete'

way indicates that *it should be read with the same kind of thinking* in which it was originally thought and written, for only then can its content be read and thought truly. At first this seems an obvious and absolute prerequisite for understanding any book—so obvious that one does not pause for thought. Yet how can this consonance be possible when the author has used super-logical (i.e. heart-) thinking to think and write the book—although he has of course then translated it into logical thinking and the German language so that it can be read at all—whereas the reader reads only in normal language, understanding what is said only through logical thinking? By means of these sentences Rudolf Steiner tried to make the reader aware that his book should be read in a different way from other books if the most important aspects are to be discovered. For these are concealed within the book. If the reader does not recognize them, he/she will only read and understand the book in an imperfect way—which is why the word 'complete' is emphasized.[9]

The word 'conversation' provides the second key to answering our question and points to the right and complete way of reading. Whoever can read the book in this way will be able *to enter into conversation* with the author, in the full sense of this wonderful word.[10] A prerequisite for such conversation, in absolute distinction to a mere discussion, is consonance between conversing partners in the form of communication and in the capacity for spiritual connection: the shared endeavour towards the goal of the conversation, trust in the common intention, certainty in mutual understanding, souls opened one to another—a *heart to heart conversation*. This is how one should regard a conversation between the spiritual student and Rudolf Steiner, which can only come about when both partners apply the same kind of thinking, the same heart-thinking. The spiritual pupil who reads the book in a 'proper and complete' way will be able to enter into a conversation with Rudolf Steiner, giving rise to the possibility of receiving from him further illumination about the book's content, as well as 'personal instruction'. At this moment, the seeming contradiction is resolved.

If one reads *How to Know Higher Worlds* in the same way that one reads other books—of course one can also read other books with all seriousness, intensity, devotion and attention—then it will remain a general, theoretical, esoteric treatise. But if one reads it *differently* it will open the way to a real conversation with Rudolf Steiner, in a form that of course corresponds with the spiritual development of each individual reader.

★   ★   ★

Bridge Building

In this book I have tried to show that the six exercises occupy a special place, different from that of all other exercises for enlivening the chakras, as well as all main exercises, meditations, etc. They are more central to the renewed esoteric path of schooling than any other exercises by virtue of the fact that they continually create anew the right framework or structure, the mood or inner stance necessary for following it. One can thus recognize in them a particular quality, one that reveals a special connection with the new esoteric path. The heart-thinking used by the spiritual teacher to form these exercises is precisely what the spiritual student can gain for the further development and deepening or elevation of his/her thinking consciousness, when he or she either can or wills to take the decisive step from the renewed ancient path of schooling to the new path represented by *The Philosophy of Freedom*. To further this possibility, Rudolf Steiner reworked the book for its second edition, prefacing the actual content of the book with 'basic exercises' of a certain kind. Referring back to the path of schooling in *How to Know Higher Worlds*, he deeply imbued the *six paragraphs* of the 'Preface to the Revised Edition' (of the second and final version of *The Philosophy of Freedom*) with a metamorphosed form of the *six* basic exercises—thus creating a formal link between the chief texts of the two esoteric paths of schooling.

———————

Notes

Editor's note: Due to the sometimes inadequate and incomplete nature of the translations of Rudolf Steiner's works in English, where necessary new translations have been made by Matthew Barton from the original German. In these cases reference is given to the relevant 'GA' (*Gesamtausgabe*, i.e. Steiner's collected works) edition. Where published translations are known to exist, this information has been added in brackets for the reader's information.

Part One, Chapter 1 (pages 3–14)

1. In German: *die sieben Wesensglieder.*
2. It is difficult properly to translate into English the title of Rudolf Steiner's book *Die Philosophie der Freiheit.* This difficulty has been succinctly outlined by Michael Wilson in connection with his translation of the book (*The Philosophy of Freedom*, Rudolf Steiner Press, London 1964). In the introduction to his translation he suggests that the German *Freiheit* could be 'rendered literally as "freehood" if such a word existed in English' but stops short of using it in the title. Since I find Wilson's argument clear and convincing, I think the time has come to introduce the word 'freehood.' Here is the passage from Wilson's 'Introduction':

'Freedom is not an exact equivalent of the German word *Freiheit*, although among its wide spectrum of meanings there are some that do correspond. In certain circumstances, however, the differences are important. Steiner himself drew attention to this, for instance, in a lecture he gave at Oxford in 1922, where he said with reference to this book:

> Therefore today we need above all a view of the world based on *Freiheit*—one can use this word in German, but here in England one must put it differently because the word "freedom" has a different meaning—one must say a view of the world based on spiritual activity, on action, on thinking and feeling that arise from the individual human spirit. [Translated from the German.]

'Steiner also drew attention to the different endings of the words; *Freiheit* could be rendered literally as "freehood" if such a word existed. The German ending -*heit* implied an inner condition or degree, while -*tum*, corresponding to our -"dom", implied something granted or imposed from outside. This is only partly true in English, as a consideration of the words "manhood", "knighthood", "serfdom", "earldom", and "wisdom" will show. In any case, meanings change with time, and current usage rather than etymology is the best guide.

'When describing any kind of creative activity we speak of a "freedom of style" or "freedom of expression" in a way that indicates an inner conquest of outer restraints. This inner conquest is the theme of the book, and it is in this sense that I believe the title *The Philosophy of Freedom* would be understood today. When Steiner questioned the aptness of this title, he expressed the view that English people believed that they already possessed freedom, and that they needed to be shocked out of their complacency and made to realize that the freedom he meant had to be attained by hard work. While this may still be true today, the alternative he suggested is now less likely to achieve this shock than is the original. I have not found that the title "The Philosophy of Spiritual Activity" gives the newcomer any indication that the goal of the book is the attainment of inner freedom. Today it is just as likely to suggest a justification of religious practices. Throughout the book it has proved quite impossible to translate *Freiheit* as "spiritual activity" wherever it occurs. The word appears in the titles of the parts of the book and of some of the chapters; the book opens with the question of freedom or necessity, and the final sentence (page 218) is "He is free." Undoubtedly "freedom" is the proper English word to express the main theme of the book, and should also appear in the book's title. Times have changed, and what may well have been good reasons for changing the title in 1922 are not necessarily still valid. After much thought, and taking everything into account, I have decided that the content of the book is better represented today by the title *The Philosophy of Freedom*. Moreover, with this title the book may be instantly identified with *Die Philosophie der Freiheit*, and I have already remarked that this edition is intended as a close translation of the German, rather than a new book specially written for the English.'

I would add to Wilson's concerns that Steiner's suggestion in 1922 to use the paraphrase 'spiritual activity', although it might have been appropriate then, is no longer valid. The various meanings the word 'spiritual' has taken on, especially through the New Age Movement and the interest in eastern spirituality, are not consonant with Steiner's intentions.

3. In GA 55, p. 173. (*Supersensible Knowledge*, Anthroposophic Press, New York 1987, lecture X.)

4. The use of the term 'I' is subject to the principle of 'uncertainty' mentioned above. The true 'I' itself never manifests, but can only be grasped through its effects, through its activity manifested in the four realms of the physical, etheric, astral and ego. One can therefore distinguish between different forms of the 'I' in the following ways. As higher self, the 'I', the eternal individuality, cannot be grasped directly but only experienced intuitively. This 'I' encompasses the higher, purely spiritual bodies of spirit-self, life-spirit and spirit-man. The ego-organization consists of

the 'three souls' (sentient soul, mind soul and consciousness soul) upon which the 'I' most immediately works, and through which it further extends its activity in astral body, etheric body and physical body. The ego body appears as a 'negative body' in relation to the other three 'positive' bodies. The ego-level consists of the totality of all the aspects described above.

Part One, Chapter 2 (pages 15–27)

1. Valerie Hunt, *Infinite Mind*, Malibu, CA, 1995.
2. Barbara Ann Brennan, *Hands of Light*, New York 1988.
3. Sharamon and Baginski, *The Chakra Handbook*, Wilmot, WI, 1991, p. 25.
4. Brennan, p. 48.
5. Sharamon and Baginski, *The Chakra Handbook*, op. cit.
6. There are a few modern esotericists who have understood the difference between these two paths. The path for awakening the kundalini that is right for our times, the 'Christos' or 'Christos path', is in contrast to the old path. The necessity and the decisive role of a new kind of thinking seems, however, not to have been recognized as yet. A comparison of these two paths can be found in *Beyond the Light*, by P.M.H. Atwater, New York 1995.

Part One, Chapter 3 (pages 28–35)

1. Rudolf Steiner, *How to Know Higher Worlds*, Anthroposophic Press, New York 1994, p. 111.
2. Ibid., p. 110.
3. Ibid., p. 133.
4. Ibid., p. 132.
5. Ibid., p. 133.
6. Ibid., p. 133.
7. Ibid, p. 116.
8. Ibid, p. 118, footnote.
9. Ibid, p. 130.

Part One, Chapter 4 (pages 36–51)

1. *How to Know Higher Worlds*, p. 111.
2. C.W. Leadbeater, *The Chakras*, The Theosophical Publishing House, Wheaton, IL, Madras and London 1972.
3. *How to Know Higher Worlds*, p. 119.
4. GA 161, p. 243ff.
5. GA 94, p. 70.
6. GA 266, I, p. 100.
7. GA 119, p. 286. (*Macrocosm and Microcosm*, Rudolf Steiner Press, London 1985, lecture XI.)
8. GA 217, p. 148. (*The Younger Generation*, Anthroposophic Press, New York 1976, lecture X.)
9. GA 26, p. 62. (*Anthroposophical Leading Thoughts*, Rudolf Steiner Press, London 1973, p.53ff.)
10. GA 266, I, p. 112.
11. *How to Know Higher Worlds*, pp. 139–40.
12. *Flensburger Hefte* 51, Flensburg 1995.

Part One, Chapter 5 (pages 52–58)

1. The German term *Nebenübungen* is the plural of *Nebenübung* which is a combination of *neben* and *Übung*. The preposition *neben* means 'by, by the side of, beside, alongside of, side by side, next to, close by, near to' or 'synchronous, simultaneous, at the same time, together'; the noun *Übung* means 'exercise, practice'. *Thus the exact meaning is: exercises to be done together with or at the same time as other exercises.* When the German volume in which these exercises appeared for the first time was published in English with the title *Guidance in Esoteric Training* the term 'subsidiary' was used, in my view erroneously, to translate *Nebenübungen*. The term 'subsidiary' has led unfortunately to the *misleading assumption* that these exercises are of lesser importance than or subsidiary to other more important or main exercises. While many who work with them call them by other names (for example: accompanying, supplementary, six months), still the assumption has persisted that these exercises do not have the same stature as

other main exercises or meditations given by Rudolf Steiner. For the sake of consistency, I will use the term 'subsidiary' when I am referring to this usual assumption associated with them and the term 'basic' when I am referring to their new meaning and importance which I am presenting in this book.

2. For example, in the following volumes: GA 53 (public lectures); GA 94 (part translated as *An Esoteric Cosmology*, Garber, New York 1987), GA 95 (*At the Gates of Spiritual Science*, Rudolf Steiner Press, London 1986) and GA 97 (members' lectures); GA 245 (*Guidance in Esoteric Training*, Rudolf Steiner Press, London 1994), and GA 266 (lessons of the Esoteric School).

3. Cf. GA 245 (*Guidance in Esoteric Training*).

4. Ibid., pp. 18–19.

5. *The Stages of Higher Knowledge*, Anthroposophic Press, New York 1974, pp. 14–15.

6. Cf. *Guidance in Esoteric Training*.

7. Alexander Strakosch, 'Die Bedeutung des Studiums im anthroposophischen Erkenntnisweg' (The significance of study for the anthroposophical path of knowledge) in *Blätter für Anthroposophie*, Vol. 6, No. 7, July 1954.

8. GA 317, p. 154. (*Curative Education*, Rudolf Steiner Press, London 1993, lecture X.)

9. GA 156, p. 81. (*Occult Reading and Occult Hearing*, Rudolf Steiner Press, London 1975, lecture IV.)

Part Two, Chapter 1 (pages 61–63)

1. *How to Know Higher Worlds*, p. 121.

Part Two, Chapter 2 (pages 64–73)

1. Christian Morgenstern, 'Meditationen' (Meditations) from: 'Wir fanden einen Pfad ('We found a path') in *Werke und Briefe* (Works and letters), Vol. 2: Lyrik 1906–14, Stuttgart 1992. Translation of these verses by M. Barton.

2. *How to Know Higher Worlds*, pp. 120–21.

3. *The Stages of Higher Knowledge*, Anthroposophic Press, New York, second ed. 1974, p. 16.

4. Rudolf Steiner, *Occult Science—an Outline*, Rudolf Steiner Press 1969, p. 246.
5. Rudolf Steiner, *Guidance in Esoteric Training*, Rudolf Steiner Press 1994, pp. 19–20.
6. Such as: Henry Petroski, *The Pencil*, A. Knopf, New York 1993;
   Charles Panati, *Panati's Browser's Book of Beginnings*, Houghton Mifflin Co., Boston 1984;
   Michael Faraday, *Natural History of a Candle*.
7. See Part Three, Chapter 2, 'The Six Positions', pp. 137–38.

Part Two, Chapter 3 (pages 74–79)

1. *How to Know Higher Worlds*, p. 121.
2. *The Stages of Higher Knowledge*, pp. 16–17.
3. *Occult Science—an Outline*, p. 247.
4. *Guidance in Esoteric Training*, p. 20.

Part Two, Chapter 4 (pages 80–88)

1. *The Stages of Higher Knowledge*, p. 18.
2. GA 94, p. 44.
3. GA 266, p. 234.
4. *How to Know Higher Worlds*.
5. *The Stages of Higher Knowledge*, p. 17.
6. *Occult Science—an Outline*, pp. 247–48.
7. *Guidance in Esoteric Training*, p. 21.

Part Two, Chapter 5 (pages 89–99)

1. *At the Gates of Spiritual Science*, Rudolf Steiner Press, London 1970, p. 113.
2. *How to Know Higher Worlds*, p. 121.
3. *The Stages of Higher Knowledge*, p. 17ff.
4. *Occult Science—an Outline*, p. 249.
5. *Guidance in Esoteric Training*, pp. 21–22.
6. *The Stages of Higher Knowledge*, p. 17ff.
7. *Guidance in Esoteric Training*, p. 21.
8. GA 93a, p. 148.

Part Two, Chapter 6 (pages 100–106)

1. *How to Know Higher Worlds*, pp. 121–22.
2. *The Stages of Higher Knowledge*, p. 18.
3. *Occult Science—an Outline*, pp. 249–50.
4. *Guidance in Esoteric Training*, p. 23.
5. Ibid.

Part Two, Chapter 7 (pages 107–114)

1. *How to Know Higher Worlds*, p. 121.
2. *Stages of Higher Knowledge*, p. 18.
3. *Occult Science—an Outline*, p. 250.
4. *Guidance in Esoteric Training*, pp. 23–24.
5. *Theosophy*, chapter 'The Path to Knowledge'.

Part Two, Chapter 8 (pages 115–126)

1. The quotations taken from the volume *Aus den Inhalten der esoterischen Stunden* ('From the esoteric lessons'), GA 266, I, consist of notes written down from memory by members of the audience.
2. *Guidance in Esoteric Training*, p. 20.
3. GA 266, I, p. 418.
4. Ibid., p. 232.
5. Ibid, p. 202.
6. *Guidance in Esoteric Training*, p. 20.
7. GA 266, I, p. 233.
8. Ibid., p. 202.
9. *Guidance in Esoteric Training*, p. 21.
10. GA 266, p. 418.
11. Ibid., p. 233.
12. Ibid., p. 203.
13. *Guidance in Esoteric Training*, p. 22.
14. GA 266, I, p. 418.
15. Ibid., p. 233.
16. Ibid., p. 203.
17. *Guidance in Esoteric Training*, p. 23.
18. GA 266, I, p. 419.

19. Ibid., p. 234.
20. Ibid, p. 203.
21. Ibid, p. 419.
22. Cf. Kenneth Ring, *Towards Omega*, New York 1985.

Part Two, Chapter 9 (pages 127–132)

1. See GA 13 (*Occult Science*) for first quote; GA 245 (*Guidance in Esoteric Training*) for the second, and GA 266 for the rest.
2. *Guidance in Esoteric Training*, p. 14.
3. GA 266, I, p. 417.
4. Rudolf Steiner, *Aus den Inhalten der esoterischen Stunden* ('From the contents of the esoteric classes'), GA 266.
5. Rudolf Steiner, GA 95 (*At the Gates of Spiritual Science*, Rudolf Steiner Press, London 1986).
6. *Die Stufen der höheren Erkenntnis* ('The stages of higher knowledge'), GA 12, p. 27ff. See also Part Three, Chapter 4 in this book.

Part Three, Chapter 1 (pages 135–136)

1. *Macrocosm und Microcosm*, Rudolf Steiner Press, London 1968, p. 151ff.

Part Three, Chapter 2 (pages 137–140)

1. Rudolf Steiner, *Eurythmy as Visible Speech*, Rudolf Steiner Press, London 1955, lecture of 12 July 1924 (GA 279).
2. Belbéoch, Marc, A propos du 'Je pense la parole' et des six exercises d'harmonisation de e'âme. In *Rudolf Steiner, Les six exercises*, Chatou, undated, Les Trois Arches.
3. See note 1 above.
4. Werner Barfod, *Ich denke die Rede ... Leitsatzübung der Eurythmie* ('I think speech ... the guiding principles of eurythmy'), Dornach 1993.

Part Three, Chapter 4 (pages 154–164)

1. Rudolf Steiner, *Curative Education* (GA 317). Lecture of 5 July 1924 in Dornach.

2. *Anweisungen für eine esoterische Schulung* (GA 245).
3. See note 1 above.
4. See also the similar description of the human sheaths in *Curative Education* (GA 317), in a lecture given on 30 June 1924.

Part Four, Chapter 1 (pages 167–171)

1. I use the term used by Rudolf Steiner, 'heart-thinking', as a technical term in order to refer to the fundamentally new kind of thinking developed by him. This is a thinking which uses the heart instead of the brain as its physical organ; it differs from the normal, logical thinking and goes above and beyond it; it could thus be called 'super-logical' in the same way that 'supersensible' means above and beyond the senses. In order to be expressed through language, heart-thinking must be adapted to the neurological processes of the brain and thereby 'translated' into normal, logical thinking.
2. Rudolf Steiner, *Learning to See into the Spiritual World*, Anthroposophic Press, New York, 1990, pp. 10–11.
3. Rudolf Steiner, lecture of 29 March 1923 in Vienna, in *Macrocosm and Microcosm*, Rudolf Steiner Press, London 1968, p. 165.
4. Julie Klima, 'Erinnerungen an Rudolf Steiner' ('Recollections of Rudolf Steiner') in: Ludwig Poltzer-Hoditz, *Erinnerungen an Rudolf Steiner*, Dornach 1985.
5. Andrej Belyj, *Verwandeln des Lebens* ('Life transformation'), Basel 1975.

Part Four, Chapter 2 (pages 172–178)

1. *The Philosophy of Freedom*, tr. Michael Wilson, Rudolf Steiner Press, 1979. The work has also been published under the following titles:
The Philosophy of Spiritual Activity, tr. H. Collison, G.P. Putnam & Sons 1922;
The Philosophy of Spiritual Activity, tr. William Lindemann, Mercury Press, New York 1986;

The Philosophy of Freedom—A Philosophy of Spiritual Activity, tr. Rita Stebbing, Rudolf Steiner Press 1992; revised as *The Philosophy of Spiritual Activity—A Philosophy of Freedom*, 1992. *Intuitive Thinking as a Spiritual Path—a Philosophy of Freedom*, tr. Michael Lipson, Anthroposophic Press, New York 1995.

2. Rudolf Steiner, *Occult Science—an Outline*.
3. Rudolf Steiner, *The Course of My Life* (GA 28).
4. Rudolf Steiner, *Anthroposophische Gemeinschaftsbildung*, GA 257 (*Awakening to Community*, Anthroposophic Press, New York 1974) lecture of 6 February 1923.
5. Rudolf Steiner, *Geistige Wirkenskräfte in Zusammenleben von alter und junger Generation*, GA 217 (*The Younger Generation*, Anthroposophic Press, New York 1984). A lecture given in Stuttgart on 12 October 1922, from 'the pedagogical course for young people'.

Part Four, Chapter 3 (pages 179–187)

1. Rudolf Steiner: *How to Know Higher Worlds*, p. 108.
2. Rudolf Steiner, *Die Stufen der höheren Erkenntnis* (*The Stages of Higher Knowledge*, chapter 1).
3. In *Die Stufen der höheren Erkenntnis* and in various other contexts.
4. From the 'Second Appendix' of *The Philosophy of Freedom* (translated by M. Barton).
5. Rudolf Steiner: *Wege und Ziele des geistigen Menschen. Lebensfragen im Lichte der Geisteswissenschaft* ('Paths and goals of the spiritual human being. Life questions in the light of the science of the spirit'), GA 125. Lecture of 31 October 1910 in Berlin.
6. Ibid, GA 125. Lecture of 17 October 1910 in Basel.
7. Friedrich Rittelmeyer, *Meditation*, Floris Books, Edinburgh, p. 10.
8. Rudolf Steiner, *How to Know Higher Worlds*, p. 213.
9. Though not in the American edition cited.
10. 'Gespräch' in German, which has a resonance of direct speech and communication not wholly contained in its usual translation 'conversation'. [Translator.]

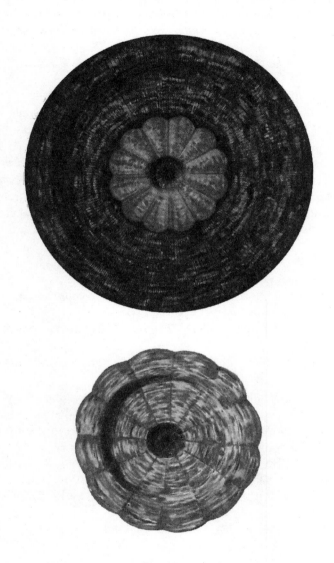

Crown chakra (above), and heart chakra (below) (after Leadbeater)